# *iOS 26 User Guide for Beginners*

### Easy Instructions, Big Text, and Colorful Helpful Photos

Lauren Klauser

*Details matter, it's worth waiting to get it right.*

- Steve Jobs

# Table of Contents

## **WELCOME TO YOUR IOS 26 USER GUIDE**

This book was created to make your journey with Apple's latest operating system simple and stress-free. Learning a new system update can sometimes feel overwhelming, but it is also exciting to see what your device can do with iOS 26. Whether you are new to iPhone or just want to feel more confident with the upgrade, you are in the right place.

This guide gives you patient, step-by-step help that builds your skills and confidence. It uses large print that is easy on the eyes and clear pictures that illustrate key steps along the way. There is no confusing tech language here. Each page gently walks you through iOS 26 on your iPhone so you always know what to do next.

You will learn how to use the core features of iOS 26, from making calls and sending texts to setting up privacy tools and using the latest upgrades across your apps. You will see how to personalize your device, capture better photos, and use simple fixes that save time and reduce stress.

By the end, you will see that iOS 26 is not just software. It is the key that makes your iPhone more helpful, more secure, and more enjoyable in everyday life.

So take a deep breath, turn the page, and get ready to explore — iOS 26 will soon feel natural and simple, like a trusted companion built right into your device.

**Please Note:** iOS 26 introduces many advanced features and gives you access to millions of apps. While no single book can cover everything, this guide focuses on the most useful tools and updates to help you get started with confidence.

Think of this book as your calm guide, almost like having a patient, tech-savvy friend by your side. Each section focuses on one part of iOS 26 on your iPhone, starting with the basics like updating your device, unlocking the Home Screen, and exploring the new layout and controls. As you move forward, you will discover how to make calls, send messages, browse the internet, use apps, and explore the new tools Apple has added in iOS 26.

Clear, large images appear throughout the book to match what you will see on your screen. You can keep the book open next to your iPhone and follow along step by step, tapping exactly what you see in the visuals.

Navigate at your own speed. You can begin at the start or skip directly to the sections that interest you most, such as learning the camera, setting up widgets, protecting your privacy, or adjusting new settings. You can repeat the steps as often as you like until they feel natural. There is no rush.

By the end, you will be using iOS 26 on your iPhone with confidence — moving easily between apps, keeping your data safe, sharing photos, staying connected with family, and enjoying the new features built into Apple's latest update. Take your time and enjoy the process. With the right guidance, even the latest software becomes simple.

### What Is iOS?

iOS is the software, also called an operating system, that runs on your iPhone. You can think of it as the "brain" of your phone. It controls how apps open, how you make calls, how your home screen looks, and how you stay safe online. Apple updates iOS every year to make your iPhone more useful, secure, and enjoyable. The latest version is iOS 26.

### Which iPhones Work with iOS 26?

Not every iPhone can run iOS 26. It works on newer models, starting with the iPhone 11 and later, as well as the iPhone SE (2nd and 3rd generations). That includes:

- iPhone 11, 11 Pro, 11 Pro Max
- iPhone 12 mini, 12, 12 Pro, 12 Pro Max
- iPhone 13 mini, 13, 13 Pro, 13 Pro Max
- iPhone 14, 14 Plus, 14 Pro, 14 Pro Max
- iPhone 15, 15 Plus, 15 Pro, 15 Pro Max
- iPhone 16, 16 Plus, 16 Pro, 16 Pro Max, 16e
- iPhone 17, 17 Pro, 17 Pro Max, iPhone Air
- iPhone SE (2nd and 3rd generations)

*Tip:* Some features may not work on all iPhones. Your apps and options may also vary depending on your region, language, and carrier.

### Main Features in iOS 26

Here are the updates that make iOS 26 different from earlier versions:

### New Lock Screen

The clock on your Lock Screen adjusts its position to keep your photo's subject visible. When you tilt your phone, the wallpaper comes alive with a 3D effect.

### Home Screen Updates

App icons now have a fresh look. You can tint them with colors or choose light, dark, or clear styles.

### Apple Intelligence

This is Apple's new set of smart tools. You can:

- Create a custom emoji called Genmoji.
- Make unique backgrounds for Messages.
- Translate texts and phone calls live.
- Use visual intelligence to learn about objects on your screen.

### Simpler Camera Design

Photo and Video modes are easier to reach, and all the controls — like flash, timer, and styles — are grouped in one spot.

### Smarter Phone App

New features help you manage calls:

- **Call Screening** lets you see who is calling before you answer.
- **Hold Assist** waits on hold for you and notifies you when it's time to return.

### Improved Messages

- Messages from unknown numbers are filtered separately.
- You can add fun backgrounds to chats.
- Group chats let you create polls and send money with Apple Cash.

### Better Photos App

The Photos app is easier to use. You can switch between *Library* and *Collections*, reorder collections, pin favorites, and choose from different display sizes.

### Smarter Maps

Maps learns your favorite routes. You can also see places you've visited and share them with friends.

### New Games App

Keep track of your games, get recommendations, and start challenges with friends in one place.

### Accessibility Features

- **Braille Access** makes iOS easier for Braille users.
- **Vehicle Motion Cues** help reduce motion sickness.
- You can temporarily use your Accessibility settings on another device.

### Family Setup

Parents setting up a phone for children ages thirteen to seventeen can enable automatic protections.

### CarPlay Upgrade

CarPlay now has a cleaner design, with new widgets, Live Activities, and easier ways to reply to messages while driving.

### Weather Alerts

Add weather widgets to your Smart Stack and get alerts for severe weather at your destination.

### Why Upgrade to iOS 26?

- A more personal Lock Screen and Home Screen.
- Smarter ways to message, translate, and stay connected.
- Tools that save time, like Hold Assist and Snap Camera controls.
- Safer browsing, stronger privacy, and better accessibility.
- Fun extras like Genmoji, AutoMix in Music, and new Maps tools.

With iOS 26, your iPhone is not just updated — it feels smarter, safer, and more enjoyable to use. This book will guide you through each of these features step by step so you can make the most of your device.

# 1. GETTING STARTED WITH iOS 26

## 1.1 TURNING ON YOUR iPHONE OR UPDATING TO iOS 26

### Starting with a New iPhone

If you've just bought a new iPhone, the setup process is simple. There's no need for you to install anything on your own. Once you turn it on, your iPhone will guide you through each step on the screen.

Here's what you'll see and do:

### The Hello Screen

Press and hold the **Side Button** until you see the Apple logo. After a few seconds, you'll see a friendly **"Hello"** message in different languages.

Swipe up from the bottom of the screen to begin.

**Accessibility Tip:** If you are blind or have low vision, you can turn on **VoiceOver** (a screen reader) or **Zoom** (to make items larger).

- To turn on **VoiceOver**, press the **Side Button** three times quickly.
- To turn on **Zoom**, double-tap the screen with three fingers.

If your iPhone doesn't turn on, plug it in for a few minutes to charge the battery. (We will learn about it in Section 1.2, *Charging Your iPhone*).

### Connect to the Internet

Your iPhone needs an internet connection to complete setup. You can use **Wi-Fi** or cellular data (mobile internet from your carrier).

Here's how to connect to Wi-Fi:

1. Choose your **Wi-Fi network name** from the list on the screen.
2. Type in the password.
3. When you see a blue checkmark    next to the name, you're connected.

### Tips

- If Wi-Fi doesn't connect right away, check your router. The network name and password are often printed on the back of it.
- If a family member already has an iPhone or iPad connected to Wi-Fi, they can share the password with you automatically when your device is nearby.

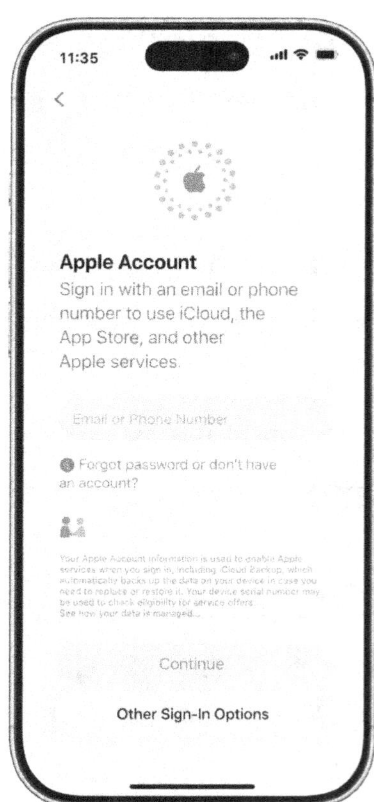

### Sign in with Your Apple Account

Next, sign in with your **Apple Account** (also called your **Apple ID**). This is the main account that connects you to all Apple services. It's what you use to download apps from the App Store, store your photos in iCloud, back up your device, and use FaceTime or iMessage to stay in touch with family and friends.

When prompted, enter your Apple ID email and password. If you have used an iPhone, iPad, or Mac before, you likely already have one. If you don't, tap **"Create Apple ID"** and follow the simple on-screen steps to make a new one. You'll need to:

1. Enter your name and date of birth.

2. Create a secure password you can remember.
3. Set up recovery options, such as a phone number or security questions, to help you sign in if you forget your password.

*Tip:* Your **Apple ID** keeps your data private. Apple doesn't share your information, and only you can access your account.

### Add a Card to Apple Pay (Optional)

You can add a debit or credit card to use **Apple Pay**, which allows secure payments in stores, apps, and websites.

- Tap **Add Card** during setup and follow the instructions.
- You can also choose **Set Up Later in Wallet** if you want to skip this step.

### Transfer Data from Another Device

You can easily move your contacts, apps, and photos from your old phone.

Here are your options:

### From another iPhone or iPad:
- Place your old and new devices close together.
- Follow the prompts to copy data and settings.
- Keep both devices plugged into power until the transfer is done.

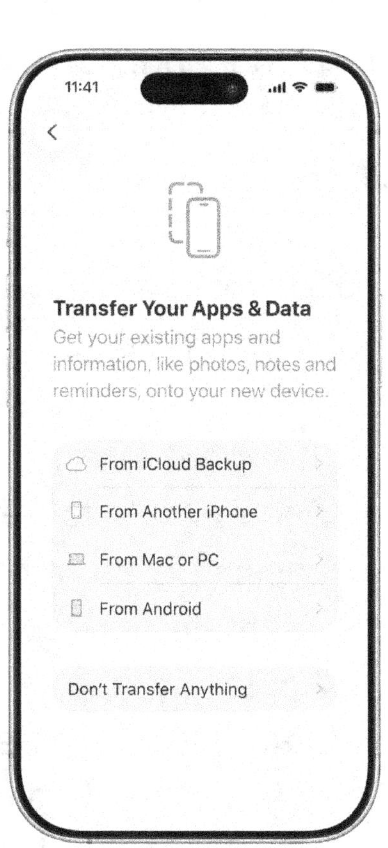


### From an Android phone:
- Download the **Move to iOS** app from the Google Play Store.
- Follow the on-screen instructions on both devices to move contacts, photos, and messages.

### From a backup:
- If you've saved a backup to iCloud or your

computer, you can restore it during setup.

*Tip:* If you want a clean start, choose **Set Up as New iPhone**. You can always add apps later.

### Set Up Face ID or Touch ID

iOS 26 supports **Face ID** and **Touch ID** by unlocking your phone and confirming payments. **Face ID** uses your face to recognize you, while **Touch ID** uses your fingerprint. Both make your phone secure and let you unlock it quickly without typing a passcode.

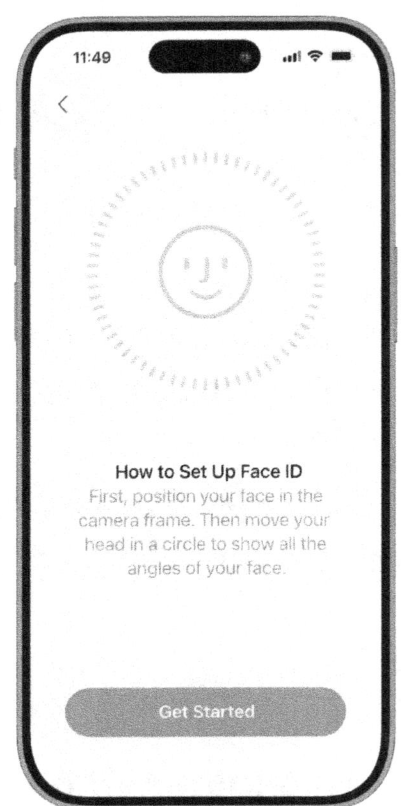


### To set up Face ID:

1. Hold your iPhone at eye level.
2. Move your head slowly in a circle so the camera can scan your face.

### To set up Touch ID:

Place your finger on the Home button.
Lift and rest it repeatedly until your fingerprint is saved.

*Tip:* Your Face ID or Touch ID data stays safely inside your iPhone and never leaves your device.

### To change it later:

- **Face ID:** Go to Settings, then select Face ID & Passcode, and enter your passcode. From here, you can Reset Face ID, Set Up Face ID again, add Alternate Appearance, and choose where Face ID is used (iPhone Unlock, Apple Pay, App Store, Password AutoFill).
- **Touch ID:** Go to **Settings → Touch ID & Passcode → Add a Fingerprint**, or tap an existing fingerprint to **rename** or **delete it**. You can also choose where Touch ID is used.

### *Turn On Find My iPhone*

Find My iPhone helps you locate your phone if it's lost or stolen.

1. Go to **Settings → [your name] → Find My→ Find My iPhone**.
2. Turn it on.

You can then see your iPhone's location using the **Find My** app or by visiting **iCloud.com**.

### *Choose Text and Icon Size*

During setup, you can adjust how big text and icons appear.

- Slide the bar to preview different sizes.
- Tap **Continue** when you find one that's easy to read.

**Tip:** You can change this anytime later in **Settings → Display & Brightness → Text Size**.

### *Updating to iOS 26*

If you already own an iPhone and want to upgrade to iOS 26, the steps are simple.

### *Check for Updates Automatically*

1. Open the **Settings app**.
2. Tap **General → Software Update**.
3. Tap **Automatic Updates**.
4. Turn on **Download iOS Updates** and **Install iOS Updates**.

Your iPhone will download updates overnight when it's charging and connected to Wi-Fi.

### Check for Updates Manually
1. Go to **Settings → General → Software Update**.
2. Your iPhone will show the current version and any available update.
3. If you see iOS 26, tap **Download and Install**.

### Update Using a Computer
You can also update through a Mac or Windows computer.

### Connect Your iPhone to Your Computer
Use the charging cable that came with your iPhone to connect it to your computer.

- You can connect your iPhone to a **Mac** with **OS X 10.9 or later**, or to a **Windows PC with Windows 7 or later**.
- Plug one end of the cable into your iPhone and the other into a **USB port** on your computer.
- If your computer doesn't have the right port, you may need a **USB adapter** (sold separately).

**Note:** When you connect your iPhone, you may see a message on your screen that says **"Trust This Computer."** Tap **Trust** to continue. This allows your iPhone and computer to communicate safely.

- On a Mac (macOS 10.15 or later): Open **Finder**, select your iPhone, then click **General**.
- On a PC (or older Mac): Open **iTunes**, click the **iPhone** icon, then click **Summary**.
- Click **Check for Update**, then **Update** if available.

**Tip:** Always use the latest version of iTunes if you're updating through your computer.

### *System File Updates Only*

If you want smaller updates without installing the full new version:

1. Go to **Settings** → **General** → **Software Update** → **Automatic Updates**.
2. Turn off **Automatically Install iOS Updates**.
3. Under **System Files**, turn on **Automatically Install**.

This keeps your iPhone running smoothly between major updates.

**Important Note:** If your iPhone is owned or managed by a school or a company, your setup process might be slightly different. Contact your administrator for help.

Now your iPhone is ready to use with iOS 26. Whether this is your first iPhone or an upgrade, you've successfully set up your device and learned how to stay updated. You're now ready to explore your Home Screen, open your favorite apps, and start discovering all the exciting new features of iOS 26.

# 1.2 Charging Your iPhone

### About Your iPhone Battery

Your iPhone uses a built-in **lithium-ion battery**. This type of battery is light, charges quickly, and lasts longer than older battery types. It also provides more power in a smaller size, giving your iPhone extended battery life.

Lithium-ion batteries charge in two stages:
- **Fast charging** until about 80%.
- **Slow (or trickle) charging** after that to protect battery health.

These steps happen automatically, so you don't need to change any settings.

### Charging with a Cable

The easiest way to charge your iPhone is with the cable that comes in the box.

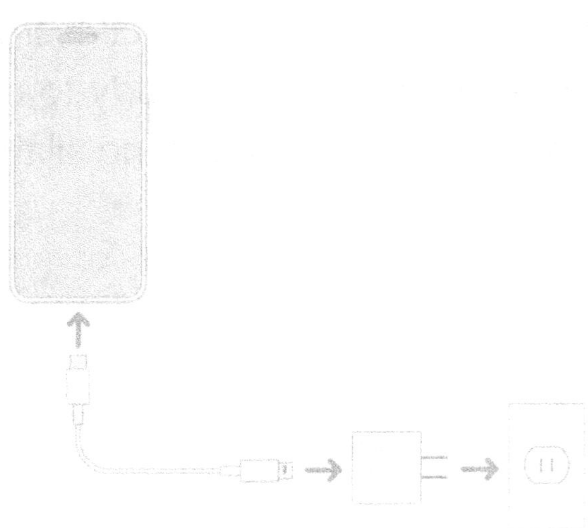

1. Plug the small end of the USB-C cable into the **charging port** at the bottom of your iPhone.
2. Plug the other end into **a power adapter** (such as the Apple 20W USB-C adapter) and connect it to a wall outlet.
3. You'll see a **lightning bolt icon** inside the battery symbol on your screen — that means your iPhone is charging.

If your iPhone battery is very low, you might see an image of an almost empty battery. This means it needs a few minutes of charging before it turns on. Plug it in and wait about ten minutes.

**Tip:** If the battery icon turns **red**, plug in your charger soon — your iPhone is running low.

### Fast Charging

Your iPhone supports fast charging. With a ***40W adapter*** or higher, it can reach up to ***50% charge in about twenty to thirty minutes***. These stronger wall chargers are sold separately but are very useful for quick top-ups.

### Charging Wirelessly

All iPhones with iOS 26 also support wireless charging, making it easy to power up without plugging in a cable.

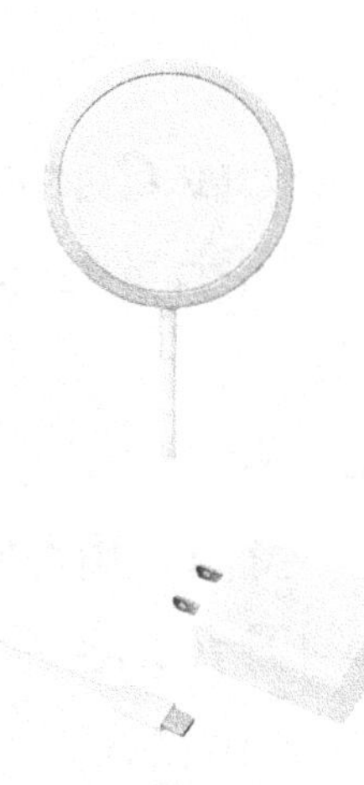

You can use:

- ***MagSafe Charger (up to 20W):*** It magnetically attaches to the back of your iPhone for a fast and secure charge.
- ***Qi-certified chargers (up to 15W):*** These work with all iPhone 8 and newer models.

To charge wirelessly:
1. Place your iPhone face up on the charger.
2. Make sure the charger is plugged into power.
3. The charging icon will appear on your screen.

**Care Tip:** Keep the charger and the back of your iPhone clean and dry. Dust or moisture can slow charging or cause heat.

You can find Qi-certified chargers in many public places like cafés, hotels, and airports.

### Charging Through a Computer

You can also charge your iPhone by connecting it to a computer.

1. Use your charging cable to connect your iPhone to a ***Mac (OS X 10.9 or later)*** or ***Windows PC (Windows 7 or later)***.
2. Make sure your computer is ***turned on*** — if it's off, your iPhone may lose power instead of charging.

3. Look for the **charging icon** on your screen to confirm that charging has started.

### Notes

- If an alert appears asking, "Trust This Computer?," tap **Trust**. This lets your iPhone safely connect to the computer.
- Avoid charging from a keyboard or low-power USB port, as it may not give enough power.

### How Charging Works

Your iPhone automatically manages charging to protect your battery:

- **Fast Charging to 80%:** Charges quickly to get most of the power in a short time.
- **Trickle Charging after 80%:** Slows down to prevent heat and extend battery life.
- **Temperature Control:** If your phone gets too hot or too cold, charging will pause until it returns to a safe temperature.

These protections happen automatically to keep your battery healthy for years.

### Battery Health and Charging Tips

All batteries lose a bit of capacity over time, but with good habits, yours will last longer.

- Keep your battery between **20%** and **80%** most days.
- Avoid letting it reach **0%** too often.
- Use **Optimized Battery Charging** to extend battery life. This feature learns your charging routine and pauses charging at 80%, finishing just before you unplug your iPhone.
  - Go to **Settings → Battery → Charging**, and turn on **Optimized Battery Charging**.

- You can also set a **Charge Limit** (like 80% or 90%) to protect your battery from overcharging.

## Set a Charge Limit

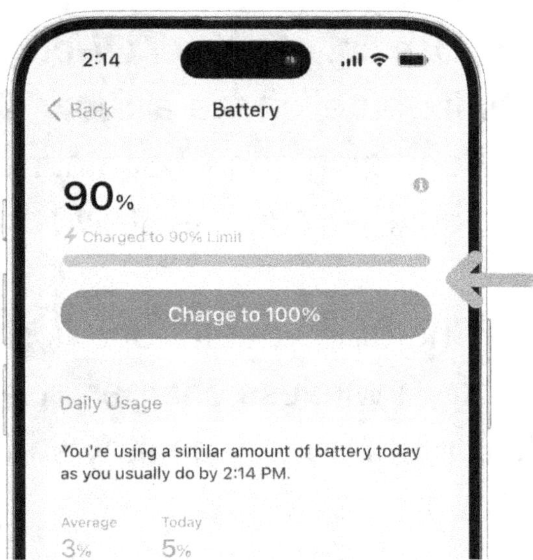

1. Open the **Settings app** ⚙ on your iPhone.
2. Tap **Battery**.
3. Tap **Charging**.
4. Choose the charge percentage that works best for you (like 80% or 90%).
5. You can change or remove the limit anytime if needed.

**Note:** Even with a charge limit set, your iPhone may occasionally charge to 100% to keep battery readings accurate.

## Check Your Battery Percentage

You can always see how much charge is left:

- Look at the battery icon in the top-right corner.
- Go to Settings → Battery and turn on Battery Percentage.
- Swipe down from the top-right corner to open Control Center, a quick-access menu that shows controls for Wi-Fi, 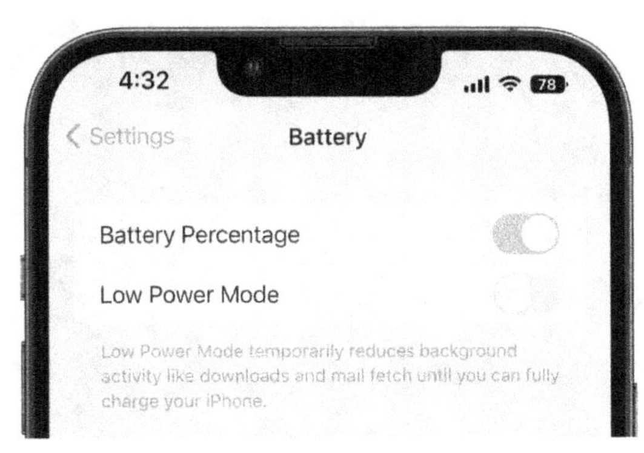 brightness, volume, and other shortcuts — including your exact battery percentage.

You can also add a Battery widget to your Home Screen or Lock Screen for quick viewing. We will learn about widgets in Sections 2.1, *The Lock Screen*, and 2.2, *The Home Screen*.

### *Important Safety Notes*

- Never charge your iPhone if the **charging port is wet**. Wait until it's fully dry.
- Use only Apple or **Qi-certified chargers** that meet safety standards.
- If you ever see a **Slow Charger** message, your iPhone supports faster charging than your current adapter can provide. Try using a stronger charger, such as 20W or higher.

Charging your iPhone is simple once you know the basics. You can use a cable, a wireless charger, or even your computer. With the right habits, you'll keep your battery healthy and strong for years to come.

## *2.1 THE LOCK SCREEN*

Your iPhone is more than a phone — it's something you can make your own. With iOS 26, Apple gives you many ways to personalize how your *Lock Screen* looks and works.

### What Is the Lock Screen?

The *Lock Screen* appears the moment you wake your iPhone. It shows the *time*, *date*, and *notifications*, and can also display *widgets* for quick information like weather, reminders, or your calendar.

In iOS 26, Apple redesigned the Lock Screen to feel more alive and personal.

### *New in iOS 26:*

- The *time* now moves around your photo so it never covers the main subject.
- Lock Screen photos include a *3D depth effect*, where the subject (like a person or pet) appears in front of the clock.
- You can *create multiple Lock Screens* and switch between them easily — for example, one for work and another for personal time.

### Customizing the Lock Screen

You can make your Lock Screen reflect your style, mood, or routine. iOS 26 lets you adjust everything — from wallpapers and fonts to widgets and effects.

### *Two Ways to Customize*

### *1. From the Lock Screen itself:*

1. Wake your iPhone by pressing the *Side Button*.
2. Touch and hold the Lock Screen until you see *Add New* ⊕ or *Customize*.
3. Tap *Add New* ⊕ to create a fresh *Lock Screen*, or *Customize* to edit

your current one.

## 2. From the Settings app:

1. Open **Settings**. 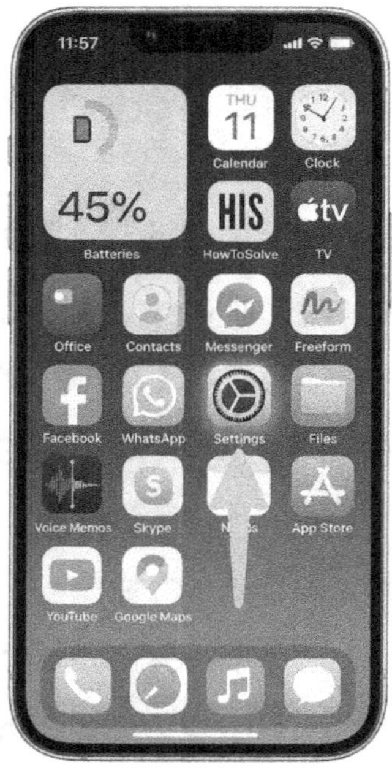
2. Tap **Wallpaper**.
3. Choose the **Lock Screen** you want to edit and tap **Customize**.

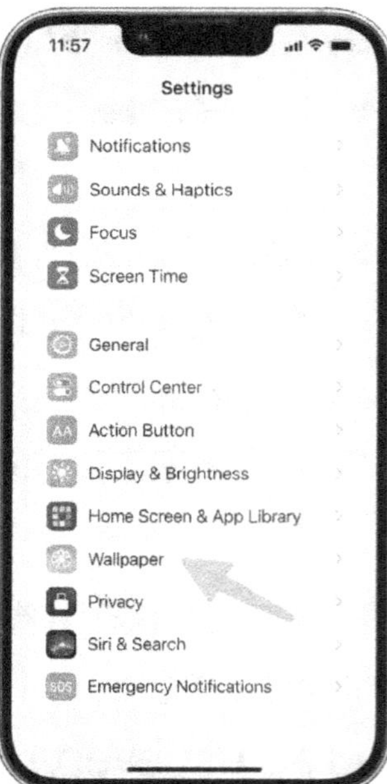

**Tip:** Using the Settings app is helpful if you prefer menus instead of gestures.

### What You Can Change

### Wallpaper

Wallpaper is the image or background that appears on your iPhone's Home and Lock screens.

- Choose from Apple's gallery, solid colors, gradients, or your own photos.
- You can also select **Live Photos** that move when you wake your iPhone.

### *What Are Live Photos?*

Live Photos are short moving pictures that capture a few seconds of motion and sound before and after you take a photo. When you press and hold a Live Photo on your screen, it comes to life like a mini video.

### *What Are Widgets?*

Widgets are small tools that show live information right on your Lock Screen or Home Screen — like the current weather, your next calendar event, battery level, or reminders. They let you see updates at a glance without opening an app.

### *Date Widget at the Top*

- Tap the date to replace it with another widget, such as **Calendar**, **Reminders**, or compatible third-party apps.

### *Clock Style and Size*

- Tap the clock to change its **font**, **color**, or **thickness**.
- Pinch with two fingers to adjust the size.

### *Widgets Below the Clock*

- Tap the space under the clock to add widgets like **Weather**, **Battery**, **Calendar**, or **Reminders**.
- To remove one, tap the **minus icon** ⊖.

### *Depth Effect*

- On supported photos, turn on **Depth Effect** to let your wallpaper's subject overlap the clock for a layered 3D look. A supported photo is one where your iPhone can clearly distinguish the subject (like a person, pet, or object) from the background.

### Light or Dark Mode

- Tap **Appearance** ◑ and choose **Light**, **Dark**, or **Auto** (which changes based on the time of day).

### Motion Effect with Live Photos

- When choosing a Live Photo, tap the **Live Photo** ◉ button to make it animate when your phone wakes.

### Filters and Colors

- Swipe left or right to apply color tones, filters, or effects.

### Saving Your Lock Screen

When you're happy with your changes:

1. Tap **Done** in the top-right corner.
2. Choose **Set as Wallpaper Pair** if you want your Lock Screen and Home Screen to match.
3. Or tap **Customize Home Screen** to create a different look for it.

### Linking Your Lock Screen to Focus

### What Is Focus?

Focus helps you manage distractions by filtering which notifications and apps can reach you. You can set different Focus modes — like **Work**, **Personal**, or **Sleep** — to control what you see and hear during different times of your day.

Examples:

- **Work Focus:** Only allows messages and emails from coworkers.
- **Sleep Focus:** Mutes everything except alarms.
- **Personal Focus:** Keeps work apps quiet but lets family messages come through.

**New in iOS 26:** You can link your Focus to your Lock Screen. When you activate a Focus, your wallpaper and widgets can change automatically to match it.

### How to Set Up Focus

1. Open the **Settings** app.
2. Tap **Focus**.
3. Choose one of the built-in options — Do Not Disturb, Personal, Work, or Sleep.
4. Or tap the **Add** ✛ button to create your own (for example, *Fitness*, *Reading*, or *Gaming*).
5. Give it a name, color, and icon.

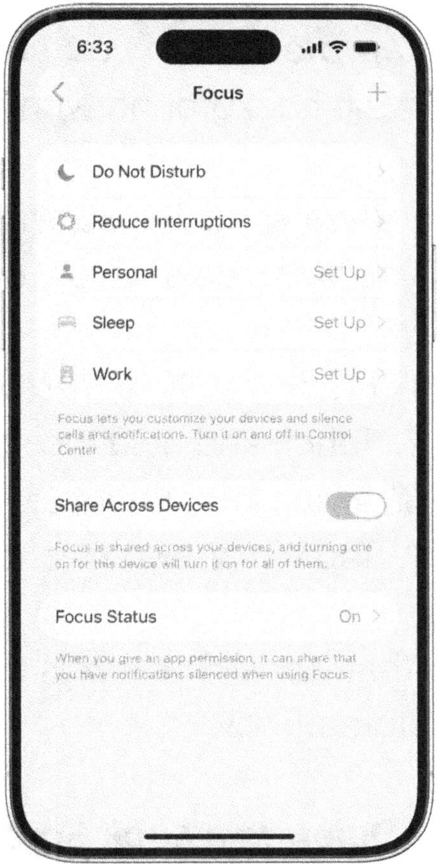

### Customize Your Focus

- **People:** Allow or silence calls and messages from specific contacts.
- **Apps:** Decide which apps can send notifications.
- **Options:** Dim the Lock Screen or hide alerts while Focus is on.
- **Schedules:** Have Focus turn on automatically by time, location, or app.
- **Filters:** Narrow down what apps show — like only work emails during Work Focus.

### Linking a Lock Screen to Focus

To connect a Lock Screen to a Focus mode:

1. Wake your iPhone and touch and hold the Lock Screen.
2. Tap **Focus** at the bottom.
3. Choose the Focus you want to link (for example, Work, Personal, or Sleep).
4. Tap **Close** to save it.

Now, when you turn on that Focus, your iPhone will automatically switch to the linked Lock Screen.

***Example:*** When you start Work Focus, your wallpaper might change to a simple background with a calendar widget and fewer notifications.

### *Switching Between Lock Screens*

If you've made several **Lock Screens**, you can switch between them easily:

1. Press the **Side Button** to wake your iPhone.
2. Touch and hold the screen.
3. Swipe left or right to browse your options.
4. Tap the one you want to use.

If that **Lock Screen** is linked to a Focus mode, the Focus will also change automatically.

### *Deleting a Lock Screen*

If you no longer need a Lock Screen:

1. Wake your iPhone and touch and hold the screen.
2. Swipe to the **Lock Screen** you want to delete.
3. Swipe up and tap the **Trash icon** 🗑, then tap **Delete This Wallpaper** to confirm.

Or go to **Settings → Wallpaper**, choose the Lock Screen, and delete it there.

With iOS 26, your Lock Screen is more personal and flexible than ever. Whether you use it to check the weather, stay focused at work, or enjoy a favorite photo, your iPhone can look and feel exactly how you want — every time you wake it up.

## 2.2 The Home Screen

The **Home Screen** is where you'll spend most of your time on your iPhone. It's the main area where all your **apps**, **folders**, and **widgets** appear. With **iOS 26**, Apple gives you more ways than ever to personalize your Home Screen and make your phone feel like it truly belongs to you.

### What Is the Home Screen?

**The Home Screen** is the first screen you see after unlocking your iPhone. It displays your apps, folders, and widgets so you can open everything with a single tap.

### New in iOS 26:

- You can **tint app icons** with colors that match your wallpaper.
- Switch icons between **light**, **dark**, or **clear** styles.
- Make icons **larger** (hiding app names) or **smaller** (keeping names visible).
- Arrange your apps and widgets anywhere you want for a layout that fits your needs.

**Note:** Some visual features, such as icon tinting and clear icon styles, may only be available on newer iPhone models like the iPhone 17 series.

### Customizing Your Home Screen

Once you unlock your iPhone, you can easily change the look and layout of your Home Screen.

Here's how:

- Go to your **Home Screen**.
- Touch and hold the background until the apps start to **wiggle**.
- Tap Edit at the top, then tap **Customize**.

Now you can adjust your Home Screen in several ways:

- **Change icon size:** Tap **Large** ◻▮ to make apps bigger (app names disappear). Tap **Small** to keep them at their normal size.

- **Tint icons:** Tap **Tinted**, then use the sliders to add color to your icons and widgets.
- **Light or Dark look:** Choose **Light** for a bright look, **Dark** for nighttime, or Auto to let your iPhone switch automatically.
- **Clear icons:** Tap **Clear** to make your icons slightly see-through.

**Tip:** These changes only affect how your Home Screen looks — they don't change how your apps work.

Add a color tint to the icons

### Widgets on the Home Screen

Home Screen widgets can be placed anywhere among your apps. You can even stack **multiple widgets** in one spot (called a **Smart Stack**) and swipe through them.

**Example:** Add a **Music widget** to control your songs or a **Calendar widget** to see your next meeting.

### How to Add a Widget

1. Touch and hold the background until apps start to wiggle.
2. Tap the **Add Widget +** button.
3. Browse or search for the widget you want.
4. Swipe through available sizes (small, medium, large).
5. Tap **Add Widget**, then drag it to where you want it.
6. Tap **Done** when finished.

### Turning an App into a Widget

Some apps can turn directly into widgets, letting you see updates without opening them.

Here's how:

1. Touch and hold an app icon on your **Home Screen**.
2. When a small menu appears, tap one of the widget size options (small, medium, or large).
3. The app turns into a widget instantly.
4. To move it, drag it while the apps are still wiggling.
5. To switch it back to a regular app icon, touch and hold it again, then tap the **app icon button** (the small icon on the left in the pop-up).

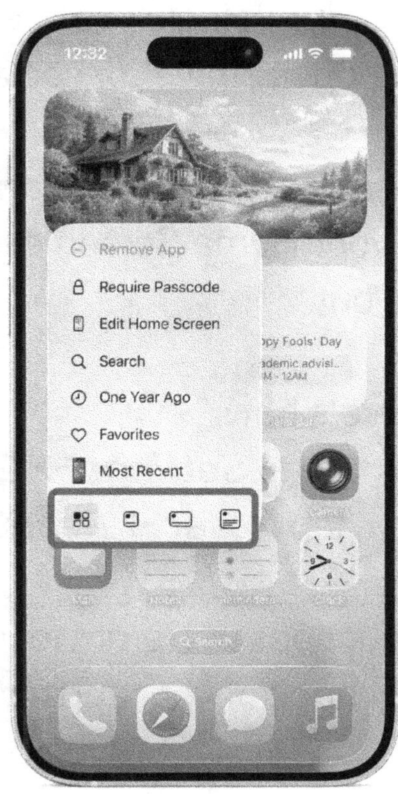

**Note:** Not all apps support this feature, but most built-in Apple apps — like Weather, Notes, and Music — do.

### *Moving Apps and Widgets*

You can move apps and widgets anywhere on your screen to keep things organized.

*To move them:*

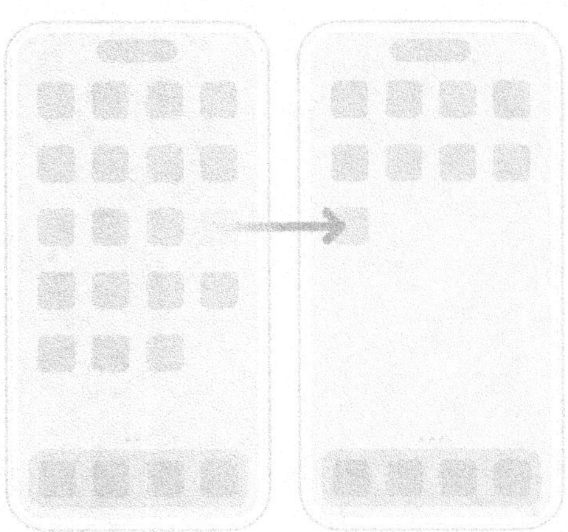

- Drag an app or widget to another spot on the same page.
- Drag it to the right edge to move it to another Home Screen page.
- Create folders by dragging one app on top of another.

*To create a folder:*

1. ***Touch and hold*** any app until all the icons start to ***wiggle***.
2. Drag one app on ***top of another*** you want in the same group.
3. A folder will appear automatically with both apps inside.
4. Tap the folder name to ***rename it*** (for example, "Games" or "Work").
5. Tap anywhere outside to stop editing.

*Tip:* Folders are great for grouping similar apps together — like all your shopping, travel, or social apps.

### Resetting Your Home Screen

If your Home Screen ever feels cluttered, you can reset it back to the original layout.

Here's how:
- Go to **Settings → General → Transfer or Reset iPhone**.
- Tap **Reset → Reset Home Screen Layout**.

Your apps will return to their original order. Folders you created will be removed, but none of your apps will be deleted.

Your Home Screen is more than just a page of apps — it's your personal space. With iOS 26, you can adjust icon colors, change layouts, add widgets, and make everything match your daily routine. Whether you use an iPhone 11, iPhone 16, or the new iPhone 17, your iPhone will look and feel like it's truly yours.

Your iPhone's **Control Center** is like a quick toolbox for your most-used features. Instead of opening the **Settings app** every time, you can swipe once and instantly access controls for Wi-Fi, brightness, flashlight, or music. Some newer iPhone models, such as the **iPhone 16e**, **iPhone 15 Pro** and **15 Pro Max**, and all **iPhone 17 models**, also include a special **Action Button** on the side. This button gives you fast access to one specific task of your choice, such as opening the camera or turning on the flashlight.

### Using Control Center

Control Center helps you reach key settings in seconds.

- To open it, **swipe down** from the **top-right corner** of the screen (where the battery icon is).
- To close it, **swipe up** from the bottom of the screen or tap anywhere outside the menu.

**Tip:** Control Center is available from almost any screen, even while using another app, unless you disable it (see the subsection *Controlling Access in Apps* below).

### Common Controls You'll Find

Control Center includes many small icons for everyday tools. Here are the most common ones:

✈ **Airplane Mode** — Turns off all wireless connections while flying.

📶 **Wi-Fi** — Connects your iPhone to the internet through a Wi-Fi network.

🔵 **Bluetooth** — Connects your iPhone to wireless headphones, speakers, or car systems.

🌙 **Focus/Do Not Disturb** — Silences calls and notifications when you need quiet time.

🔕 **Silent Mode** — Mutes all sounds on your phone.

🔦 *Flashlight* — Turns your camera flash into a light.

🔘 *AirDrop* — Quickly shares photos or files with nearby Apple devices.

*Tip:* Some controls show more options when you touch and hold them.

For example, press and hold **Camera** to choose between *Selfie*, *Video*, or *Portrait* — so you can jump straight into what you need without opening the full Camera app.

Touch and hold to
see Camera options

You can try this with other controls too:

- *Flashlight:* Press and hold to adjust the brightness level.
- *Wi-Fi or Bluetooth:* Touch and hold to see nearby networks or connected devices.
- *Music:* Press and hold to view the full playback screen with song details and controls.

Exploring these hidden options helps you save time and makes your iPhone feel even easier to use.

### Turning Off Your iPhone from Control Center

You can also power off your iPhone right from Control Center.

While Control Center is open, **touch and hold the Power button** ⏻ in the top-**right corner** of the screen until you feel a light vibration. A slider will appear — **drag it to the right** to turn off your iPhone.

### *Customizing Control Center*

You can set up Control Center to show only what you need most. Add, remove, or rearrange controls so they fit your daily routine.

To customize Control Center:
1. Open **Control Center**.
2. Tap **Add a Control** to add a new one (like Screen Recording or Low Power Mode).
3. To remove one, tap the **minus** ⊖ icon beside it.
4. To rearrange, drag the three lines next to any control to move it up or down.

**Example:** Add the **Magnifier** control so you can zoom in on small print, such as menus or medicine labels, with a single tap.

### *Wi-Fi and Bluetooth in Control Center*

You can manage Wi-Fi and Bluetooth connections right from Control Center.

- Tap the **Wi-Fi** icon to temporarily disconnect from your current network. Your iPhone will reconnect later when you move locations or restart it.
- Tap the **Bluetooth** icon to pause connections to devices such as AirPods.

**Note:** These buttons only **pause** connections. If you want to **fully turn off Wi-Fi or Bluetooth**, go to **Settings → Wi-Fi or Settings → Bluetooth**.

### *Adjusting Volume and Brightness*

- **To change volume:** Use the **side buttons** or open Control Center and move the **speaker slider** up or down.

- *To adjust brightness:* Open **Control Center** and drag the **sun slider** ☀
  up to make the screen brighter or down to dim it.

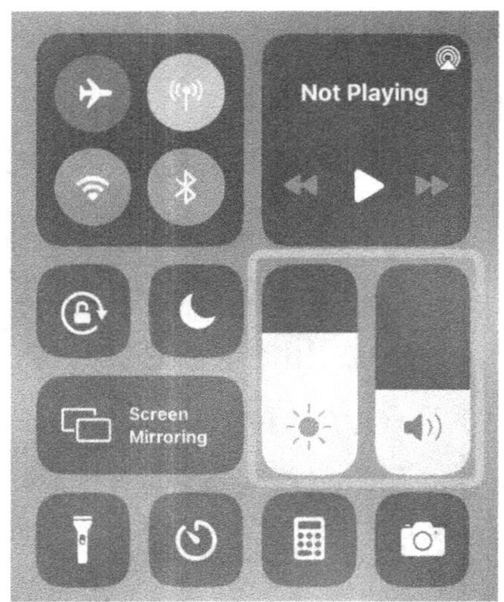

### Controlling Access in Apps

If you often open Control Center by accident while gaming or watching videos, you can turn off its use inside apps.

Here's how:
- Go to **Settings → Control Center**.
- Turn off **Access Within Apps**.

Now, Control Center will only open from your Home Screen or Lock Screen.

### The Action Button

(iPhone 16e, iPhone 15 Pro models, and iPhone 17 Series only.)

Some newer iPhone models include a special button called the **Action Button**. It sits on the **left side of the phone**, just above the volume buttons. This button replaces the old Ring/Silent switch and can be set to perform a single useful task that you choose.

### What the Action Button Can Do

You can assign one of the following actions to the button:

🔕 **Silent Mode** — Switch between ring and silent.

🌙 **Focus** — Turn on a Focus like Do Not Disturb or Work.

📷 **Camera** — Open the Camera quickly.

🔦 **Flashlight** — Turn your iPhone's light on or off.

〰 **Voice Memo** — Start a quick audio recording.

Ⓢ **Recognize Music** — Identify a song using Shazam.

⌨ **_Translate_** — Translate speech or text instantly.
⊕ **_Magnifier_** — Use your camera as a magnifying glass.
**_Controls_** — Open any control from Control Center.
**_Shortcut_** — Run a custom shortcut or open an app.
**_Accessibility_** — Quickly open features like VoiceOver or Zoom.
**_No Action_** — Do nothing (useful if you press it by accident).

Some choices require a follow-up selection. For example, if you pick **_Shortcut_** or **_Controls_**, you must choose which specific action or app to open.

### Using the Action Button
- **_Press and hold_** the button to run the task.
- Some actions work like switches — press and hold again to turn them off. For example, Silent Mode, Flashlight, and Focus all toggle on and off.
- You'll feel a gentle **_vibration_** (called haptic feedback) when your action starts.

### Setting or Changing the Action
1. Open **_Settings_**.
2. Tap **_Action Button_**.
3. Swipe through the list under the phone image and stop at the one you want.
4. If you see a **_Menu_** button under an option, tap it to choose a specific setting.

Examples:
- **_Camera_** → Choose Photo, Video, Selfie, or Portrait.
- **_Focus_** → Pick which Focus mode to toggle.
- **_Shortcut_** → Choose a specific shortcut or app.
- **_Accessibility_** → Pick one feature like VoiceOver or Magnifier.

Press and hold the Action Button to test it right away.

### Avoid Accidental Presses
If you often press the button by mistake, you have two options:

- Set **No Action**, or
- Choose something harmless like **Magnifier** instead of Silent Mode.

### Troubleshooting the Action Button

- **Nothing happens:** Go to **Settings → Action Button** and check that you selected a specific task.
- **Wrong action:** Open **Settings** again and choose a new option.
- **No sound or feedback:** You may be in Silent Mode or a Focus Mode — press and hold again to turn it off.

Control Center and the Action Button both exist to save you time. With one quick swipe or press, you can adjust brightness, take a photo, turn on the flashlight, or connect to Wi-Fi. Whether you're using an older iPhone or the newest model with an Action Button, iOS 26 keeps the most useful tools right at your fingertips.

Siri and Spotlight are your iPhone's built-in helpers. Siri listens and responds to your voice so you can make calls, send messages, play music, set reminders, check the weather, or solve math problems without touching the screen. Spotlight lets you type to search for anything on your iPhone — apps, messages, emails, photos, and even information from the web. With iOS 26, both Siri and Spotlight are faster, smarter, and ready to help you anytime.

### *Turning On Siri*

Before using Siri, make sure it's turned on:

1. Open the **Settings app**. ⚙️
2. Tap **Siri & Search** (or **Apple Intelligence & Siri** on some models).
3. Tap **Talk to Siri**.
4. Choose how you want to activate Siri:
   - **"Siri" or "Hey Siri"** — your iPhone will respond to either phrase.
   - **"Hey Siri" only** — your iPhone will respond only to "Hey Siri."
5. To use the **Side Button** instead, turn on **Press Side Button for Siri**.

> **Note:** Siri needs an **internet connection** (Wi-Fi or mobile data) for most tasks.

### *How to Activate Siri*

You can activate Siri in several easy ways:

- **With your voice:** Say "Siri" or "Hey Siri."
- **With Face ID models:** Press and hold the **Side Button**.
- **With EarPods:** Press and hold the center button on the cord.

Siri responds to a request for an alarm at 8:00 AM

Indicates that Siri is listening

- ***In your car (CarPlay):*** Hold the voice command button on your steering wheel. We will learn more about CarPlay in Chapter 10, *Navigate Smartly, Use CarPlay, and Do More.*
- ***With AirPods:*** Use voice or touch, depending on your model.

Once Siri is listening, you can ask:
- "Hey Siri, what's eighteen percent of 225?"
- "Siri, set a timer for three minutes."
- "Hey Siri, call Mom."

### Changing Siri's Voice and Language
You can change how Siri sounds and which language it uses.

1. Open **Settings → Siri & Search**.
2. Tap **Siri Voice** to pick a new voice or accent (if available).
3. Tap **Language** to select another language.

Some voices and languages may require downloading additional files — your iPhone will do this automatically when connected to Wi-Fi.

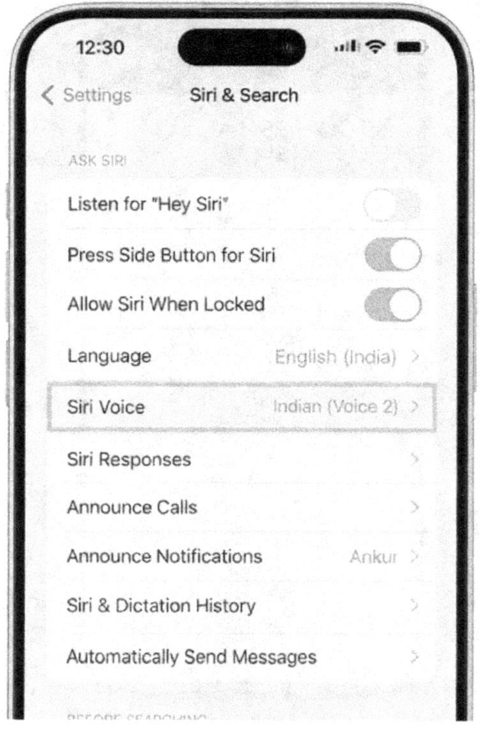


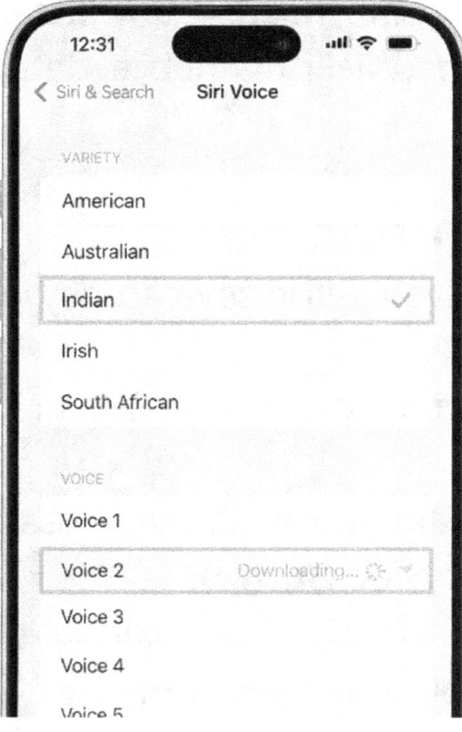

### *Adjusting How Siri Responds*

You can control how and when Siri speaks back to you.

1. Go to **Settings → Siri & Search → Siri Responses**.
2. Choose one or more of the following:
   - **Spoken Responses:** Decide when Siri replies out loud.
   - **Always Show Siri Captions:** See Siri's answers as text on screen.
   - **Always Show What You Say:** See your requests written out.

*Tip:* To make Siri wait longer while you're speaking, go to **Settings → Accessibility → Siri → Siri Pause Time** and pick **Default, Longer,** or **Longest**.

### *Managing When Siri Listens*

You can choose when Siri is allowed to respond:

- Go to **Settings → Siri & Search → Talk to Siri**.
- To stop voice activation completely, select **Off**.
- To stop Siri from working while your iPhone is locked, turn off **Allow Siri When Locked**.

This helps protect your privacy and prevents accidental activations.

### *Retraining Siri to Recognize Your Voice*

If Siri doesn't always recognize your voice correctly, you can retrain it.

1. Open **Settings → Siri & Search**.
2. Tap **Talk to Siri** and turn it **off**.
3. Turn it **back on**, then follow the on-screen setup steps to teach Siri your voice again.

### *Using Siri for Calls, Messages, and FaceTime*

Siri can help you stay connected hands-free:

- ***Hang up calls:*** Go to ***Settings → Siri & Search → Call Hang Up*** and turn it on.
- ***Send messages automatically:*** Go to ***Settings → Siri & Search → Messaging with Siri***, then turn on ***Automatically Send Messages***.
- ***Announce calls and messages:*** On supported headphones, Siri can read aloud who's calling or texting you.

***Examples:***
- "Hey Siri, text Sarah, 'I'll be there in ten minutes.'"
- "Siri, call Dad."
- "Hey Siri, FaceTime John."

### Controlling What Siri Shows in Search

You can control which apps appear when you search using Siri or Spotlight.

1. Open ***Settings → Siri & Search***.
2. Scroll down and tap an app (like Photos or Messages).
3. Turn options on or off depending on what you want Siri to include in searches.

**What this means:** This lets you choose which apps Siri can look through when showing results or suggestions. For example, if you turn it off for **Photos**, Siri won't show pictures when you search. If you leave it on, Siri can include photos, messages, or files related to what you're asking for.

### Typing Instead of Talking to Siri

If you prefer typing to speaking:

1. Go to ***Settings → Accessibility → Siri***.
2. Turn on ***Type to Siri***.
3. When you activate Siri, a keyboard will appear so you can type your request.

### *Asking Multiple Questions*

With iOS 26, you can ask Siri follow-up questions without saying "Hey Siri" again.

Example:

> "Hey Siri, what's the weather in New York?"
> "What about Los Angeles?"

If Siri misunderstands, you can:
- Tap the *Listen* button ⦻ to repeat your request.
- Spell out tricky words or names.
- Edit your question on screen using the keyboard.

### *Turning Off Siri*

If you no longer want to use Siri:

1. Go to *Settings → Siri & Search*.
2. Tap *Talk to Siri* and select *Off*.
3. Turn off *Press Side Button for Siri*.

You can turn it back on anytime later if you change your mind.

### *Searching with Spotlight*

Spotlight is another smart way to find things quickly on your iPhone. While Siri works with your voice, *Spotlight* helps you *search by typing*. You can use it to find *apps*, *contacts*, *messages*, *emails*, *photos*, *or even text inside photos* using Apple's *Live Text* feature. Spotlight can also show *web results*, *stock updates*, *and currency information* — all in one place.

### *How to Open Spotlight*

There are two easy ways to start a Spotlight search:

- On iPhones with **Face ID**, tap the Search button 🔍 at the bottom of your Home Screen.
- Or simply **swipe down** from the middle of your Home Screen or Lock Screen.

A search bar will appear at the top of your screen.

### How to Use Spotlight
1. Tap the **search bar** and type what you're looking for — like an app name, a contact, or a file.
2. Tap **Search** 🔍 on the keyboard to see results.
3. Tap any result to open it.

You can also:
- **Open a suggested app or website** directly.
- **Take quick actions** — such as starting a timer, turning on Focus Mode, or finding a song using Shazam.
- See **app shortcuts** — for example, searching "Photos" may show a shortcut to open your **Favorites album**.

**Tip:** Spotlight updates results as you type, so you can often find what you need before you finish typing the full word.

### Choosing Which Apps Appear in Spotlight
You can control which apps show up in Spotlight results.

1. Go to **Settings → Siri & Search**.
2. Scroll down and tap an app (for example, **Photos** or **Mail**).
3. Turn **Show App in Search** on or off.

**What this means:** Turning an app off hides its content from Spotlight results. For example, if you turn off "Show App in Search" for Photos, Spotlight won't show any pictures or albums when you search.

### *Turning Off Location-Based Suggestions*

Spotlight sometimes gives suggestions based on your location, such as nearby stores or restaurants. If you don't want this:

1. Go to **Settings → Privacy & Security → Location Services**.
2. Tap **System Services**.
3. Turn off **Suggestions & Search**.

### *Searching Inside Apps*

Many apps, like **Messages**, **Mail**, or **Maps**, have their own search field too.

To search inside an app:
1. Open the app.
2. Tap the **search bar** (or swipe down if you don't see one).
3. Type what you're looking for and tap **Search**. Q

### *Adding a Dictionary for Better Searches*

You can add dictionaries to help Spotlight and Siri understand more words and definitions.

1. Go to **Settings → General → Dictionary**.
2. Select one or more dictionaries you want to add.

Once added, Siri and Spotlight can give better word meanings, translations, and writing suggestions.

Siri and Spotlight work hand in hand. Siri helps you find things with your voice, while Spotlight lets you search by typing. Both can pull results from your apps, photos, emails, and the web — making iOS 26 one of the fastest and easiest systems to use.

### 3.1 Calling Essentials

Your iPhone makes calling simple. You can make, receive, and manage calls easily — plus use new iOS 26 tools that help screen unknown numbers and reduce spam. Whether you're calling family, friends, or work, your iPhone keeps you connected.

### Initiating a Call

1. Open the **Phone** app.
2. Tap the **Keypad** and enter the number.
3. Tap the green **Call** button.
4. Or tap **Contacts**, select a person, and tap the **call icon** next to their number.

**Tip:** You can also ask **Siri** — say, "Siri, call John."

### Answer a Call

- If your iPhone is **unlocked**, tap **Accept** or **Decline**.
- If it's **locked**, slide the **green slider** to the right to answer.

### Decline or Silence a Call

- Tap **Decline** to send the call to voicemail.
- Press the **Side Button once** to silence the ringtone (the caller will still hear it ringing).

### Favorites

You can save your most-used contacts as **Favorites** so you can call them quickly.

1. Open the *Phone* app.
2. Go to *Contacts*.
3. Choose a person.
4. Tap *Add to Favorites*.

*Tip:* Calls from Favorites can still come through during certain *Focus Modes* (like Work or Sleep), if you allow it in *Settings*. Go to *Settings → Focus → [select your Focus] → People → Allow Calls From → Favorites*.

### Add and Save Contacts

Add a New Contact
1. Open *Phone → Contacts*.
2. Tap the *Add* button.
3. Enter the name and number.
4. Tap *Done*.

### Save a Number You Just Dialed

After ending a call, tap *Add Number*, then choose *Create New Contact* or *Add to Existing Contact*.

### Save from Recents

1. Open *Phone → Recents*.
2. Tap the *info* button next to the number.
3. Tap *Create New Contact* or *Add to Existing Contact*.

### Wi-Fi Calling

You can make and receive calls using *Wi-Fi* when your signal is weak.

1. Go to *Settings → Cellular → Wi-Fi Calling*.
2. Turn it on.

You'll see Wi-Fi next to your carrier name when it's active.

### Dual SIM

If your iPhone uses **two lines**, you can choose which line to use before calling. Go to **Settings → Cellular** to set a default line or switch between them during calls.

### While on a Call

- Use the **volume buttons** to adjust call volume.
- Tap **Mute** to silence your voice.
- Tap **Speaker** to use the speakerphone or a headset.
- Use the **Keypad** to type a number.
- Swipe up to open another app while staying on the call.
- Tap the **green call bar** at the top to return to the call.

### Caller Identification

Your iPhone can identify who's calling using **Apple Business Connect**, your carrier, or trusted caller ID apps. Go to **Settings → Phone → Call Blocking & Identification**, then turn on any available options.

### Screening and Silencing Unknown Calls

You can now ask unknown callers to **say their name and reason for calling** before you answer — or silence them completely.

1. Go to **Settings → Phone**.
2. Choose one:
   - **Never** — rings for all calls.
   - **Ask Reason for Calling** — caller speaks before the phone rings.
   - **Silence** — unknown calls go to voicemail and appear in the Recents list.

During call screening, Siri will speak in your iPhone's language.

### *Filter Unknown and Spam Calls*

Keep unwanted numbers out of your Recents list.

1. Go to *Settings → Phone*.
2. Turn on:
   - *Unknown Callers* — moves unknown numbers to a separate list.
   - *Spam* — suspected spam calls go straight to voicemail.

### *Add a Contact to Your Known Callers List*

1. Open the *Phone* app and tap the *Filter* button.
2. Tap *Unknown Callers*.
3. Tap *Mark as Known* next to the number.

To undo this, go to Contacts, select the number, and tap Mark as Unknown.

### *Block or Unblock a Number*

*Block:*
1. Open *Phone → Contacts* and choose a contact.
2. Tap *Block Contact*.

*Unblock:*
1. Go to *Settings → Phone → Blocked Contacts*.
2. Tap *Edit*.
3. Tap *Remove* next to the number, then tap *Unblock*.

### *View Unknown or Spam Calls*

1. Open the *Phone* app.
2. Tap *Calls* (or *Recents*, depending on layout).
3. Tap the *Filter* button.
4. Choose *Unknown Callers* or *Spam*.

### *Use Hold Assist*

When a business puts you on hold, ***Hold Assist*** can wait for you and alert you when a real person comes back on the line.

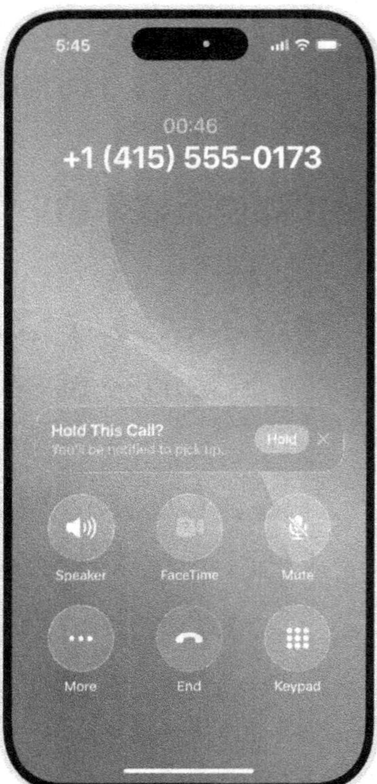

- During a call, tap ***More***. ⋯
- Tap ***Hold Assist***.
- Keep your volume on so you hear when the call resumes.

You can enable ***Hold Assist Detection in Settings →  Phone → Hold Assist Detection*** (this feature may not be available in all regions).

   Your iPhone makes calling easy and stress-free. You can manage contacts, block spam, and even let your phone wait on hold for you — all while staying connected to the people who matter most.

Texting on your iPhone is quick, safe, and fun. You can send messages to anyone, share photos, videos, or stickers, and even pay people with Apple Cash. iOS 26 also adds better tools to block spam and filter unknown senders so your inbox stays clean.

### *Messages Setup*
1. Open the *Settings* app.
2. Tap *Messages*.
3. Turn on *iMessage*.
4. Tap *Send & Receive* and choose the phone number or email you want to use.

*Blue bubbles are iMessages* — these are sent over the internet between Apple devices. They use *Wi-Fi or cellular data* and are *end-to-end encrypted*, which means only you and the other person can read them. You can also send high-quality photos, videos, stickers, effects, and even Apple Cash.

*Green bubbles are regular text messages (SMS or MMS)* — these go through your phone carrier. They work with any phone but may use your text plan and show lower-quality photos or videos. You won't see typing indicators or read receipts.

If an iMessage doesn't send, your iPhone can resend it as a regular text. To allow this, turn on *Send as SMS* in *Settings → Messages*. You can also touch and hold a blue bubble and tap *Send as Text Message*.

### *Sending a Message*

(The following actions work the same for iMessages and regular texts.)

1. Open the **Messages** app. ⭕
2. Tap the **Compose** button. ✐
3. Type a name or number, or pick a contact.
4. Type your message.
5. Tap ⊕ to add Photos or Videos, or 🎤 to dictate your message.
6. Tap the **Send Arrow** ⬆ to send.

### *Starting a Group Conversation*

You can chat with several people at once — perfect for family, friends, or work groups.

1. Open the **Messages** app. ⭕
2. Tap the **Compose** button. ✐
3. Type the names, numbers, or email addresses of the people you want to include.
4. Write your first message and tap **Send**. 

Once the group chat starts, everyone in the conversation can reply and see each other's messages.

### *Replying in a Chat*

- Tap a notification or open **Messages**, then tap the chat.
- Type your reply and tap **Send**. 

To reply to a specific message, swipe right on the message bubble, type your reply, then tap the blurred area to return to the main chat.

### Unsend or Edit a Message

- To **unsend**, touch and hold the message within two minutes, then tap **Undo Send**.
- To **edit**, touch and hold within fifteen minutes, tap **Edit**, make changes, and tap **Send Edit**.

### Chat Backgrounds

You can now personalize your chat background in iOS 26.

### Use a dynamic look:

1. Open **Messages** and choose a chat.
2. Tap the contact or group name at the top.
3. Tap **Backgrounds** → choose **Color**, **Sky**, **Water**, or **Aurora**.
4. Swipe through styles and tap **Done**. 

### Use a photo:

1. In **Backgrounds**, tap **Photo**.
2. Pick a picture, pinch to crop, and add effects like **Black & White**, **Duotone**, or **Color Wash**.
3. Tap **Done**.

### Remove or turn off:

- For one chat: go to **Backgrounds** → **None**.
- For all chats: go to **Settings** → **Messages** → **Conversation Backgrounds** and turn it off.

**Tip:** To show chat photos first when reopening a conversation or thread, go to **Settings** → **Messages** and turn on **Start with Photos Visible**.

### Share Your Name and Photo

1. Open **Messages**.
2. Tap **Edit** (or **More**) → **Name & Photo**.

3. Choose a photo or Memoji, enter your name, and select who can see it.

### *Screen and Filter Unknown Texts*

Keep messages from unknown numbers out of sight.

What filtering does:
- Sorts texts from numbers not in your contacts.
- Puts them into folders like *Transactions* (receipts, delivery updates) and *Promotions* (ads or sales).
- You won't get alerts for these unless you allow them.

### *Turn On Filtering*

1. Open *Messages*.
2. Tap the *Filter* button at the top.
3. Tap *Manage Filtering*.
4. Turn on *Screen Unknown Senders*.
5. Tap *Allow Notifications* to let some filtered messages (like codes) still alert you.

### *Auto-Sort Promos and Receipts*

In *Manage Filtering*, tap *Text Message Filter* and turn it on. You can also use trusted third-party filters.

   *Note:* Filters don't apply to senders you've replied to three times or more.

### *Reviewing Filtered Messages*

1. Open *Messages* → tap *Filter*.
2. Choose *Unknown Senders*, *Transactions*, *Promotions*, or *Spam*.

To *Mark as Known*, open a message in Unknown Senders and tap *Mark as Known*, or simply add the number to *Contacts*.

*Note:* You must mark a sender as known before you can open links they send.

### Spam and Blocking

### Check the Spam Folder
- In *Messages*, tap *Filter* 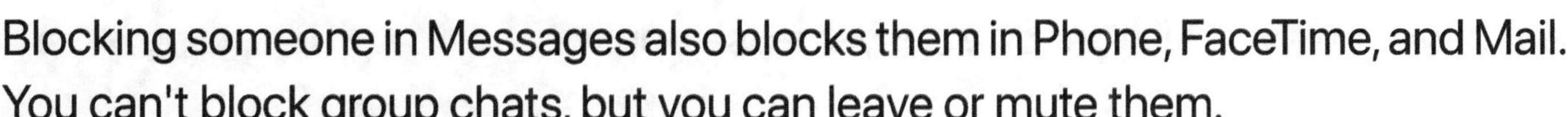 → *Spam*.
- Tap *Not Spam* to move it back.

### Report Spam
- If unopened: swipe left on the message → tap *Delete* 🗑, then *Delete and Report Spam*.
- If opened: tap *Report Spam* at the bottom → tap *Delete and Report Spam*. You can't report it after replying.

### Block a Number
1. Open the chat.
2. Tap the name at the top → *Info*. ⓘ
3. Scroll down → *Block Contact*.

### Unblock
1. Go to *Settings* → *Privacy & Security* → *Blocked Contacts*.
2. Tap *Edit*, then tap *Remove*. ⊖

Blocking someone in Messages also blocks them in Phone, FaceTime, and Mail. You can't block group chats, but you can leave or mute them.

### Apple Cash: Sending Money
You can send or request money directly inside a chat (U.S. only).

1. Open a chat.
2. Tap the *Apps* button ⊕ → *Apple Cash*.
3. Enter an amount.

4. Tap **Send** or **Request**, then **Send** again to confirm.

**Tip:** Tap an underlined dollar amount in a chat to open Apple Cash with that amount ready.

**Note:** You must have Apple Pay set up to use Apple Cash. For setup instructions, see Section 8.2, *Apple Pay*.

### Syncing Messages with iCloud
1. Go to **Settings → [your name] → iCloud**.
2. Tap **See All**.
3. Turn on **Messages**.

Now your conversations stay updated across all your Apple devices.

### Using Siri with Messages
You can use Siri to send or read texts hands-free. Try:

- "Hey Siri, send a message to Anna saying I'll be there soon."
- "Siri, read my last message."
- "Siri, reply 'Sounds good.'"

Texting in iOS 26 is simple, private, and organized. You can stay in touch with friends and family, enjoy rich iMessage features, and keep unwanted texts out of your way — all from one easy-to-use app.

## *4.1 CAMERA USAGE*

Your iPhone camera makes it easy to take clear photos and smooth videos. With iOS 26, the Camera app is faster, smarter, and simpler to use. In this section, you'll learn how to open the Camera, take great pictures, and record videos with ease.

### Different Ways to Open the Camera
You can open the Camera in several quick ways:

- Tap the **Camera** app on the Home Screen.
- On the **Lock Screen**, swipe left.
- Touch and hold the **Camera button** 📷 on the Lock Screen.
- Open **Control Center** and tap **Camera**.
- Say, **"Siri, open Camera."**
- For **supported models** (like iPhone 16 Pro, 16e, and iPhone 17), you can set the **Action Button** to open the Camera instantly.
- **On iPhone 17 models only**, you can press the side **Camera Control** to open the Camera app directly.

A small **green dot** appears in the top-right corner when your camera is in use. This lets you know it's active and helps protect your privacy.

### Taking a Photo
1. Open the **Camera**.
2. Frame your subject on the screen.
3. Tap the **Shutter button** (the white circle) or press a **Volume button** to take the photo.
4. On the iPhone 17, click the **Camera Control** button once to open the

Camera, then click it again to take a picture.

### Switching Camera Modes

You can swipe left or right to choose different shooting modes:

- *Photo* — for everyday pictures (includes Live Photos).
- *Video* — for recording moving clips with sound.
- *Portrait* — for sharp subjects and soft, blurred backgrounds.
- *Cinematic* — for videos with changing focus, like in films.
- *Pano* — for wide landscape shots.
- *Slo-mo* and *Time-lapse* — for creative motion videos.
- *Spatial* (iPhone 17 only) — for immersive 3D videos viewable in Apple Vision Pro.

*Tip:* You can keep your preferred mode as the default. Go to **Settings →
Camera → Preserve Settings** and turn on **Camera Mode**.

### Zooming In and Out

- Pinch the screen to zoom in or out.
- Touch and hold the zoom control, then drag the slider.
- Tap quick zoom steps like *0.5x*, *1x*, or higher if available on your model.

### Focusing

Focus helps your subject stay sharp and clear.

- Tap your subject on the screen to focus.
- Touch and hold to lock focus and exposure (you'll see *AE/AF Lock* appear).
- Tap again to unlock it.

### Adjusting Exposure

Exposure changes how bright or dark your photo looks.

- Drag the **sun slider** ☀ up to brighten or down to darken.
- Or swipe up and tap **Exposure** from Camera Controls ⦂⦂⦂ to adjust the level manually.

To keep your exposure settings for next time, go to **Settings → Camera → Preserve Settings → Exposure Adjustment**.

### Using Flash

You can turn the flash **on**, **off**, or **auto**:

1. Tap **Camera Controls** ⦂⦂⦂ at the top of the screen or swipe up.
2. Tap **Flash** and pick your setting.
3. To always see the Flash icon, go to **Settings → Camera → Indicators → Flash**.

### Photographic Styles

You can give your photos a consistent look using **Photographic Styles**.

1. In **Photo** or **Portrait** mode, open **Camera Controls.** ⦂⦂⦂
2. Tap **Styles** and swipe to preview options like **Rich Contrast** or Vibrant.
3. Tap **Done**, then take your photo.

### Setting a Timer

The timer lets you take hands-free photos — great for group shots or selfies.

1. Open **Camera Controls.** ⦂⦂⦂

2. Tap *Timer* and choose *3s*, *5s*, or *10s*.
3. Tap the *Shutter button* and get ready.

### Choosing Aspect Ratio

The aspect ratio changes the shape of your photo.

1. Open *Camera Controls*. ▦
2. Tap *Aspect* and pick *1:1 (square)*, *4:3 (standard)*, or *16:9 (wide)*.

### Grid and Level

These tools help you line up your photos neatly.

- Go to *Settings → Camera*.
- Turn on *Grid* to divide the screen into equal parts.
- Turn on *Level* to know when your iPhone is perfectly straight.

### Camera Control (iPhone 17 Only)

The iPhone 17 introduces a *physical Camera Control button* on the side for quick photo and video control.

- *Click once* to open the Camera app.
- *Click again* to take a photo.
- *Press and hold* to start recording a video.
- *Lightly double-press* to open the settings overlay.

In this overlay, you can slide to adjust *Exposure*, *Depth*, *Zoom*, *Cameras*, *Styles*, or *Tone*, then press select.

Slide the tip of your finger or thumb on the Camera Control to scroll through settings choices or adjust the chosen setting

Customize these options in **Settings** → **Camera** → **Camera Control** → **Customize**.

You can also:
- Lock focus and exposure in **Settings** → **Camera** → **Camera Control** → **Lock Focus and Exposure**.
- Choose whether a **single click** or a **double click** opens the Camera.

Your iPhone's camera is one of its most powerful tools. Once you know how to open it, focus, and adjust your settings, you can capture memories easily. Whether it's a quick snapshot or a cinematic video, iOS 26 makes taking great photos simple and enjoyable.

## *4.2* FINDING, VIEWING, AND SHARING PHOTOS AND VIDEOS

Your iPhone makes it easy to enjoy your favorite moments. With iOS 26, the Photos app is simple, organized, and bright. You can find pictures quickly, watch videos, and share memories with family and friends in just a few taps.

### Open Photos
1. Tap the **Photos** icon on your Home Screen.
2. Make sure **Library** is selected at the bottom left to see all your photos and videos.

### Browse Your Library
- **Scroll:** Swipe up or down to move through your photos and videos.
- **Jump by time:** Tap **Years** or **Months** to quickly move to a specific time in your life.
- **Zoom:** Pinch with two fingers to zoom in for larger previews or zoom out to see more photos at once.
- **Search:** Tap **Search** and type words like "beach," "cake," or "dog" to find photos by subject, person, or place.

### Change How the Library Looks
1. In **Photos**, tap **Sort and Filter** , then **View Options**.
2. You can then:
   - **Zoom in** or **out** to change the thumbnail size.
   - **Use the Aspect Ratio Grid** to see each photo in its original shape, or the **Square Photo Grid** for uniform tiles.
   - **Hide Screenshots** to tidy up your library.
   - **Hide Shared with You** to remove items received through Messages.
   - **Hide Shared Library Badge** to remove small icons from iCloud Shared Photo Library items.
   - **Hide From My Mac** to hide photos imported from your computer.

*Tip:* If videos and Live Photos start playing automatically, you can stop this. Tap your account icon (top right corner of Photos) and turn off *Auto-Play Motion and Loop Videos*.

### Use Collections

Collections group your memories into easy-to-browse sections such as *Memories*, *Pinned*, *Albums*, and *Recent Days*.

1. Tap *Collections* at the bottom of Photos.
2. Swipe up to scroll or swipe left or right under each heading to see more.
3. Tap a heading to open all photos or videos in that group.

### Change How Collections Look

1. Open *Collections*.
2. Tap *More Options* ⬤⬤⬤ → *Layout and Reorder*.
3. Choose a view: *Large Grid*, *Small Grid*, *Mixed Grid*, or *Collapse All*.
4. Tap *Reorder* to drag sections into a new order, then tap *Done*.
5. If you use *iCloud Shared Photo Library*, choose whether to show *Both Libraries*, *Personal Library*, or *Shared Library*.

### See People and Pets

Your iPhone recognizes faces and pets automatically.

1. Tap *Albums → People & Pets*.
2. Tap a face or pet to see all related photos.
3. Tap *Name This Person* or *Name This Pet* to label them.
4. Tap *Make Key Photo* to pick their main image.

### Share Photos and Videos

1. Open a photo or video.

2. Tap **Share**. ⬆

3. Choose how to send it — **Messages**, **Mail**, **AirDrop**, or another app.

4. To share several items, tap **Select**, choose multiple photos or videos, then tap **Share**.

### Share with AirDrop

AirDrop sends photos, videos, and files to nearby Apple devices instantly. It uses Wi-Fi and Bluetooth, so both must be on.

### To turn on Wi-Fi and Bluetooth:

1. Swipe down from the top-right corner to open **Control Center**.

2. Tap the **Wi-Fi** 🛜 and **Bluetooth** ✳ icons so they light up.

### To send with AirDrop:

1. Open the photo or video.

2. Tap **Share**.

3. Then select **AirDrop**.

4. Pick a nearby device.

5. The other person taps **Accept** to receive it.

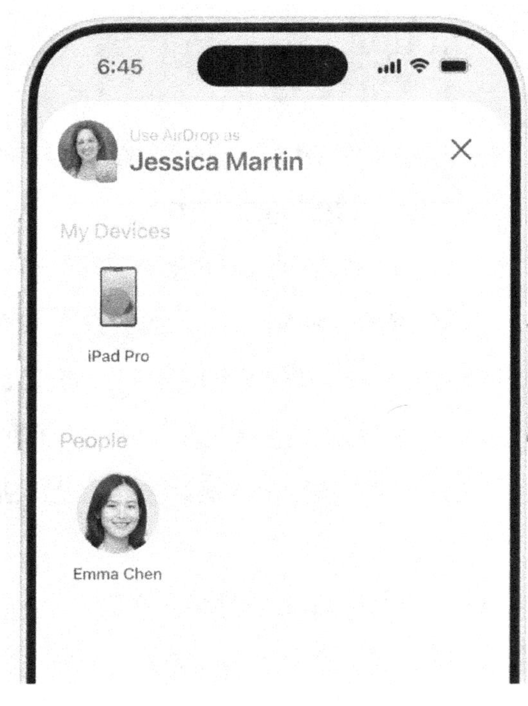


Keep devices close — within about thirty feet (nine meters). If you send something to another of your own Apple devices signed in with the same Apple ID, it usually saves automatically.

### Accept and Save with AirDrop

You can choose who can AirDrop files to you:

1. Open **Control Center**.

2. Press and hold the box that shows **Wi-Fi and Bluetooth**.

3. Tap **AirDrop** ⊚ and pick **Contacts Only** or **Everyone for ten Minutes**.

### *Save Photos Sent by Text or Email*

1. Touch and hold the photo in a message.
2. Tap **Save**.
3. Find it later in the **Photos** app.


### *Helpful Tips*

- **Make Albums:** Open **Albums**, tap the **+** button, select **New Album**, give it a name, and choose the photos you want to add.
- **Use Favorites:** Open a photo and tap the ♡ to save it in the Favorites album.
- **Stay Organized:** Hide screenshots or shared photos to keep your grid neat.
- **View on iPhone 17:** Photos look brighter and more true-to-life on the iPhone 17's advanced display.


With iOS 26, finding and sharing your photos and videos is simple. You can browse by time, location, or person, keep your library clean, and share memories with anyone in seconds.

# 5. APPLICATIONS IN THE NEW IOS 26

## 5.1 BUILT-IN APPS

Your iPhone comes ready to use right out of the box. With **iOS 26**, you get a full set of helpful apps that allow you to call, text, take photos, browse the web, stay organized, and much more.

If you're using an **iPhone 17**, these apps are already installed for you. If you're upgrading an older iPhone to **iOS 26**, most of these apps will appear automatically, but a few (like *GarageBand*, *iMovie*, or *Numbers*) may need to be downloaded again from the **App Store** — for free. (We will learn how to do that in the next section.)

You can quickly find any app by **swiping down** on the Home Screen and typing its name in the search bar.

### Communicate & Stay in Touch

 **Phone** — Make and receive calls, check voicemail, and manage contacts.

 **Messages** — Send texts, photos, videos, and iMessages (blue bubbles) securely over the internet.

 **FaceTime** — Make free video and audio calls with family and friends who use Apple devices.

 **Mail** — Read and send email; it works with iCloud, Gmail, Outlook, and more.

 ***Contacts*** — Store names, numbers, addresses, birthdays, and notes for the people you know.

## Photos, Video & Creativity

 ***Camera*** — Take sharp photos and smooth videos; switch modes like Portrait, Pano, Slo-mo, and more.

 ***Photos*** — View, edit, and organize pictures; it finds people and pets automatically and creates Memories.

 ***Clips*** — Create short, fun videos with captions, stickers, and effects.

 ***iMovie*** — Edit videos, combine clips, add music and titles for polished movies.

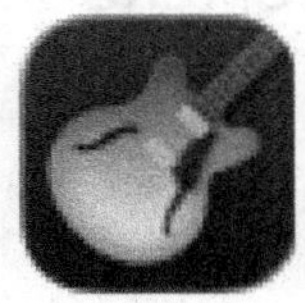 ***GarageBand*** — Make music or record instruments and voice with easy-to-use tools.

 ***Freeform*** — A blank canvas for sketching ideas, adding notes, photos, and shapes.

 ***Voice Memos*** — Record reminders, lectures, songs, or stories with one tap.

## Everyday Tools & Organization

 **Calendar** — Keep track of appointments, birthdays, and reminders; it syncs across devices.

 **Reminders** — Create to-do lists with alerts that can pop up at a time or place.

 **Notes** — Jot down lists, checklists, and ideas; add photos, scans, and drawings.

 **Clock** — Set alarms, timers, and world clocks; use the Stopwatch to track events and laps.

 **Calculator** — Do quick math; rotate the iPhone for more functions.

 **Files** — Browse and organize documents on iPhone, iCloud Drive, and other services.

 **Measure** — Use the camera to measure objects and level frames.

 **Magnifier** — Turn the camera into a digital magnifying glass with zoom and contrast options.

 **Compass** — See direction, elevation, and coordinates; handy for walks, hikes, and travel.

 **Weather** — Local forecasts, rain alerts, and air quality at a glance.

 ***Tips*** — Short how-tos that teach helpful iPhone features.

## Browse, Read & Watch

 ***Safari*** — Browse the web, save favorites, and use Reader to make pages easier to read.

 ***Books*** — Read eBooks and audiobooks; adjust text size and appearance.

 ***News*** — Follow trusted news sources and topics; customize what you see.

 ***TV*** — Watch shows and movies from Apple TV+ and other apps in one place.

 ***Podcasts*** — Discover and listen to free shows on any topic.

 ***Music*** — Play songs from your music library or, with Apple Music, stream playlists and tracks.

 ***iTunes Store*** — Buy and download music and movies to own forever.

## Get Around & Find Things

**Maps** — Turn-by-turn directions for driving, walking, transit, or cycling; explore places nearby.

**Find My** — Locate your iPhone, AirPods, Apple Watch, AirTag items, and share locations with family.

## Home & Wallet

**Home** — Control lights, locks, thermostats, and other smart-home devices.

**Wallet** — Keep credit or debit cards for Apple Pay, transit cards, event tickets, and passes.

**Watch** — Pair and manage Apple Watch settings, faces, and health data.

## Health, Fitness & Well-Being

**Health** — View health records, medications, activity, sleep, and more in one private place.

**Fitness** — Track daily activity; with Apple Fitness+ (optional), follow guided workouts.

**Journal** — Reflect with prompts and add photos, locations, and workouts to your entries.

### Shopping & Downloads

***App Store*** — Find, download, and update apps and games (many are free).

***Apple Store*** — Shop for iPhone, iPad, Mac, accessories, and book in-store appointments.

### Work & School (iWork Suite and More)

***Pages*** — Create letters, flyers, and documents (similar to Microsoft Word).

***Numbers*** — Make simple budgets and tables (similar to Microsoft Excel).

***Keynote*** — Build presentations with themes and animations (similar to Microsoft PowerPoint).

***Shortcuts*** — Automate tasks (for example, send a daily text with one tap).

### Privacy, Safety & Translate

***Passwords*** — Save and autofill passwords, passkeys, and verification codes securely (iCloud Keychain).

***Settings*** — Adjust everything: Wi-Fi, sounds, display, privacy, and more.

***Translate*** — Translate text and speech; have bilingual conversations on the spot.

### Info & Finance

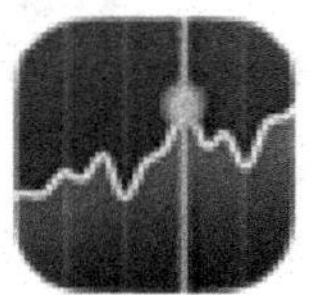

***Stocks*** — Follow markets and your watchlist; see news for each company.

### App Switcher

The App Switcher helps you jump between recently used apps or close one that's frozen.

- On iPhones with **Face ID**, swipe up from the bottom edge and pause in the middle.
- Swipe left or right to find the app you want, then tap it to open.
- To close an app, swipe it up off the screen.

### Quick How-To

- ***Open an app:*** Tap its icon on the Home Screen.
- ***Can't find it?*** Swipe down and type the name in the search bar.
- ***Move or delete apps:*** Touch and hold an icon until it jiggles, then drag or tap Remove App.

***Tip:*** You can add widgets for many of these apps — like Calendar, Weather, or Fitness — to see quick info right on your **Lock Screen** or **Home Screen**. For details, see Sections 2.1, *The Lock Screen*, and 2.2, *The Home Screen*.

With these built-in apps, your iPhone running iOS 26 is ready for everyday life — from calls and emails to photos, health, and travel — no extra setup required.

If you're using an older iPhone model, simply update to iOS 26 and download any missing apps from the App Store to enjoy the same experience. We'll learn more about this in the following section.

Your iPhone can do much more with *apps* — small programs for games, fitness, photos, travel, and daily life. The **App Store** is the safest and easiest place to find these apps. Every app is reviewed by Apple, so you can download with confidence, knowing it meets quality and privacy standards.

All iPhones running iOS 26 can use the App Store. On iPhone 17 models, downloads are slightly faster due to improved speed and Wi-Fi performance.

### Meet the App Store

The **App Store** is Apple's official shop for apps.

- Many apps are *free*.
- Some apps have a *price* or offer *in-app purchases*.
- You need an *internet connection* and your *Apple account* to download apps.

### Open the App Store

1. Tap the *blue App Store* icon on your Home Screen.
2. If you don't see it, swipe left until you reach the **App Library**, then type **App Store** in the search bar.

### Find New Apps

Inside the App Store, you'll see several tabs at the bottom:

- *Today* — See featured apps, stories, and editor's picks.
- *Games* — Explore trending and new games.
- *Apps* — Discover tools for work, creativity, and health.
- *Arcade* — Access hundreds of games with no ads (requires a subscription).
- *Search* — Type a keyword like *crossword* or *budget planner*, then tap **Search** on the keyboard.

### Check App Details

Before downloading an app, look through its details page:

- **Screenshots** and short videos show how it works.
- **Ratings and reviews** from other users.
- **Compatibility** with Family Sharing and other Apple devices.
- **App size** and **age rating**.
- **Privacy details** that explain what data the app may collect.

### Download an App

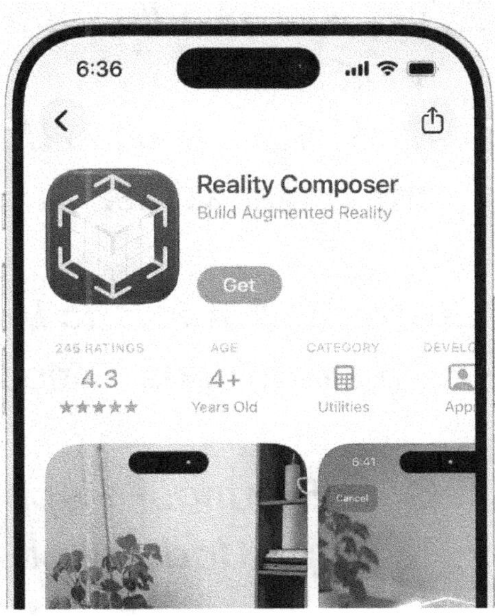


1. Tap **Get** for free apps, or tap the **price** if it's a paid app.
2. If you see a **cloud icon** ☁, that means you downloaded it before — tap it to reinstall for free.
3. Confirm with **Face ID**, **Touch ID**, or your **passcode**.
4. Wait for the circle to fill — your app will appear on the **Home Screen** or in the **App Library**.

**Tip:** You can track the download progress by watching the small circle fill around the app icon.

### Find Apps You Installed

1. Swipe to the **App Library** (last Home Screen page).
2. Tap the **search bar** at the top.
3. Type the app's name, then tap the icon to open it.

### Share or Gift an App

1. Open the app's page in the **App Store**.
2. Tap **Share**. ⬆
3. Choose **Messages** or **Mail** to send the link.

4. To **gift an app** (in supported regions), tap **Gift App** and follow the on-screen steps.

### Keep Apps Up to Date

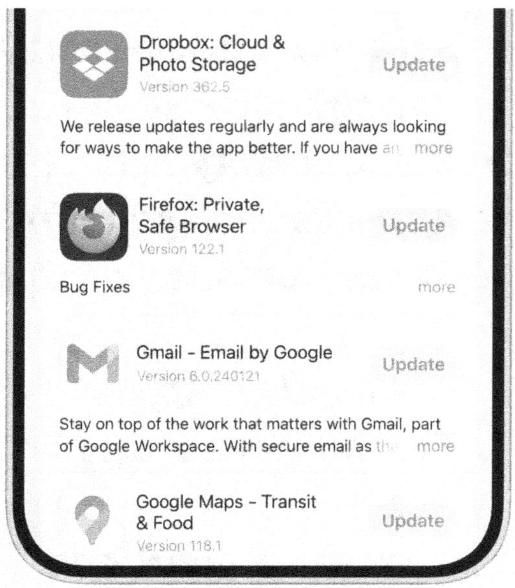


Your iPhone updates apps automatically by default.

To check or update manually:

1. Open the **App Store**.
2. Tap your **profile picture** at the top right.
3. Scroll down and tap **Update All** or update one app at a time.

### Turn Off Automatic Updates

If you prefer to update apps yourself:

1. Go to **Settings → App Store**.
2. Turn **App Updates** off.

You can still open the App Store anytime to check for updates manually.

### Remove or Offload an App

If you need to free up space:

- **To delete an app completely:**
  1. Touch and hold the app icon.
  2. Tap **Remove App → Delete App**.

- **To offload an app but keep your data:**
  1. Go to **Settings → General → iPhone Storage**.
  2. Tap the app name → **Offload App**.
  3. You can reinstall it later without losing data.

### *Family Sharing Basics*

Family Sharing lets up to six people share apps, purchases, and subscriptions safely.

What it does:
- Shares paid app purchases and eligible subscriptions.
- Shares Apple services like *Apple Music*, *TV+*, *Arcade*, *Fitness+*, and *News+*.
- Lets your family share one *iCloud+ storage plan*.
- Adds *Ask to Buy* for kids, so you approve their purchases.
- Allows you to manage *Screen Time* for children.
- Shares *locations* through *Find My* (optional).

*To set it up:*
1. Go to *Settings* → *[your name]* → *Family Sharing*.
2. Tap *Set Up Your Family* and follow the steps to invite members.
3. Choose what you want to share — you can change or stop sharing anytime.

### *Safety Tips*
- Read the *Privacy* section on each app page before downloading.
- Go to *Settings* → *Privacy & Security* to control which apps can access your *Location*, *Photos*, *Camera*, or *Microphone*.
- Download only apps from the *App Store* — never from links or outside websites.

With these simple steps, you can explore, install, and enjoy apps that fit your interests. Whether you're using an iPhone 17 or an older model updated to iOS 26, the App Store is your safe place to discover new tools, learn new things, and make your iPhone even more useful.

Your iPhone keeps your privacy in your hands. Every time an app wants to use your information — like your location, photos, contacts, camera, or microphone — it must ask first. You can allow or deny any request and change your choices later. All iPhones running iOS 26 have these privacy features.

### Control App Access to Your Information

You decide which apps can use your personal data. This includes Contacts, Photos, Calendars, Reminders, Motion & Fitness, and more.

To check or change access:
1. Open **Settings**.
2. Go to **Privacy & Security**.
3. Tap a category (for example, Photos or Contacts).
4. Turn each app's access **on** or **off**.

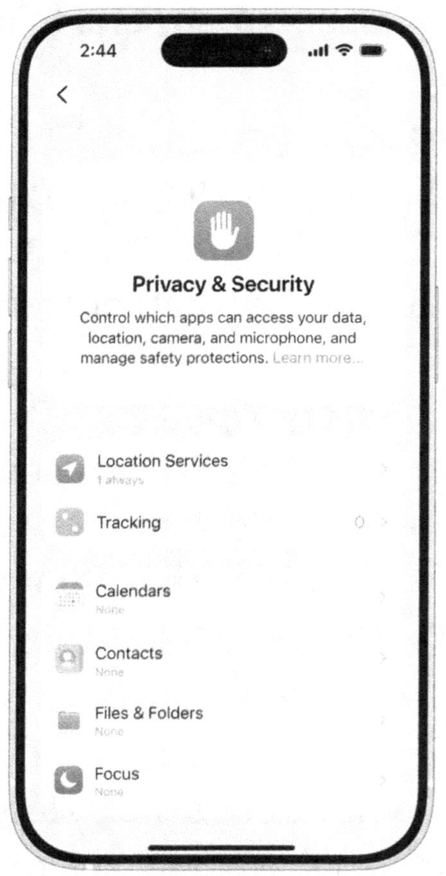


**When an app asks for permission**, a message will appear explaining why it needs access. You can choose **Allow** or **Don't Allow**. You can always change this later in the same settings.

### Understand App Permissions

The **App Privacy Report** shows how often your apps use the permissions you've given and which websites or services they contact.

To view or manage it:
1. Go to **Settings → Privacy & Security → App Privacy Report**.
2. Review how each app used your data.
3. To stop or reset the report, turn it **off** (you can turn it on again anytime).

### Location Services (and Precise Location)

Location Services helps your iPhone use GPS, Wi-Fi, Bluetooth, and cellular data to figure out where you are.

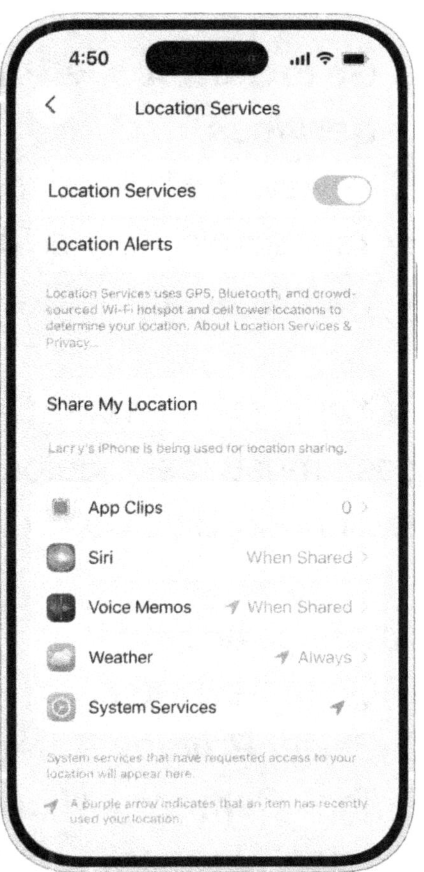

To turn Location Services on or off for all apps:
1. Go to **Settings → Privacy & Security → Location Services**.
2. Toggle **Location Services** on or off.

**Note:** Turning off Location Services completely can affect apps like Maps, Weather, and Find My iPhone.

### Control Per App
1. Go to **Settings → Privacy & Security → Location Services**.
2. Tap any app.
3. Choose **Never**, **Ask Next Time**, **While Using the App**, or **Always** (if available).
4. Toggle **Precise Location** on for exact results (for example, turn-by-turn navigation) or off for an approximate area.

### Hide the Map in Location Alerts
When an app asks to use your location, a small map may appear. You can turn this off.

1. Go to **Settings → Privacy & Security → Location Services → Location Alerts**.
2. Turn off **Show Map in Location Alerts**.

### System Services and Location
Some Apple system features also use your location, like Find My, Routing, or

Emergency Calls.

1. Go to **Settings → Privacy & Security → Location Services → System Services**.
2. Review the list and toggle each service on or off as you prefer.
3. You can also turn on the **Status Bar Icon** to see when system services use your location.

### Control Access to Camera, Microphone, and Other Hardware

Apps must ask before using your Camera, Microphone, Bluetooth, or Local Network.

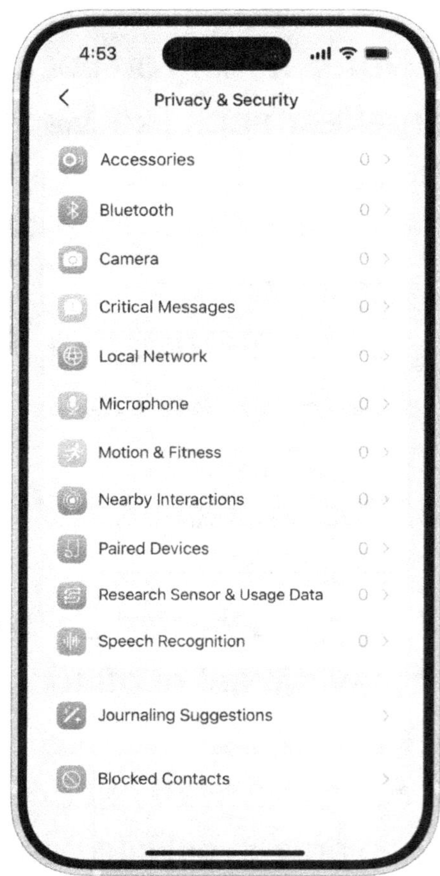

To manage access:
1. Go to **Settings**.
2. Select **Privacy & Security**.
3. Tap **Camera**, **Microphone**, **Bluetooth**, or **Local Network**.
4. Toggle each app's access **on** or **off**.

Camera and Microphone Indicators
- A **green dot** means the **camera** (or camera and microphone) is active.
- An **orange dot** means only the **microphone** is active.
- Swipe down to open **Control Center** to see which app used them most recently.

### App Tracking Permissions (Ads & Data Sharing)

Apps can't track your activity across other apps or websites unless you give permission. This reduces targeted ads and keeps your browsing private.

To control tracking:
1. Go to **Settings → Privacy & Security → Tracking**.

2. Toggle individual apps **on** or **off**.
3. To block all tracking requests in the future, turn off **Allow Apps to Request to Track**.

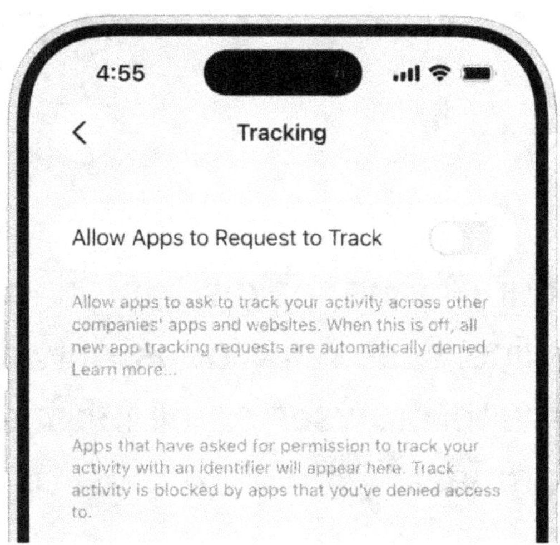


### Quick Privacy Checklist

Keep your iPhone private and safe with this simple list:

- Review your **App Privacy Report** every few weeks.
- Use **While Using the App** for most location permissions.
- Turn **Precise Location** on only when it's truly needed, like for Maps.
- Check **Camera**, **Microphone**, and **Bluetooth** access every few months.
- Turn off any app's access if you don't think it needs it — you can always re-enable it later.
- Read each app's **Privacy Policy** on the App Store page or in its permission prompt.

With these tools, you control what your apps can see and use. iOS 26 makes privacy simple — your iPhone works for you, not the other way around.

# 6. Browsing the Internet

## 6.1 Explore the Web

Your iPhone makes exploring the internet easy. You can read the news, shop online, search for ideas, or watch tutorials in just a few taps. **Safari** is the built-in web browser on all iPhones running **iOS 26**. You'll find its icon — a blue compass.

### Open Safari

1. Find and tap the **Safari** app on your **Home Screen**.
2. If you don't see it, swipe left until you reach the **App Library**, type **Safari**, then press and hold the icon and tap **Add to Home Screen**.

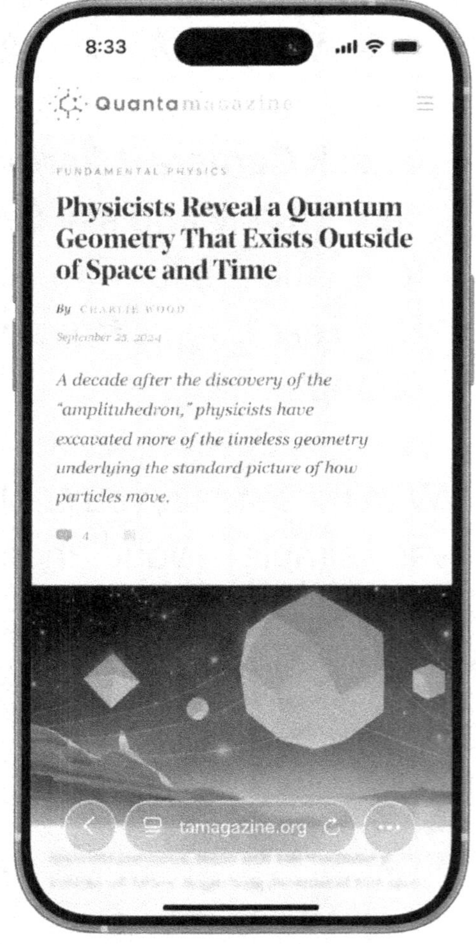


### Visit a Website

1. Tap the **address bar** (it's at the bottom by default).
2. Type a topic (for example, apple pie recipe) or a full web address (for example, bbc.com).
3. Tap **Go** on the keyboard to visit the page.

**Tip:** You can also use **Siri** and say, "Search for Italian restaurants near me."

### Handy Browsing Moves

- **Go back to the top:** Tap the status bar (very top edge of the screen).
- **Refresh a page:** Pull down on the page and let go.
- **See a wider view:** Turn your iPhone sideways to use **landscape mode**.
- **Share a page:** Tap **More Options**, then **Share** to send the link by **Messages**, **Mail**, or **AirDrop**.

### *Preview Links Safely*

If you're unsure about a link, check it first:

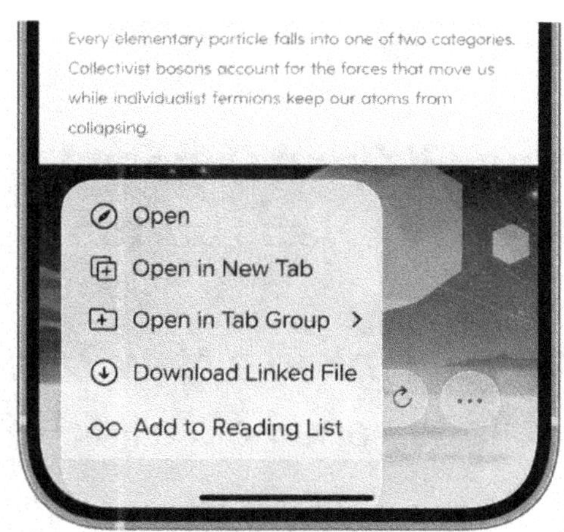


1. ***Touch and hold*** the link.
2. A small preview will appear.
3. Tap ***Open*** to visit or ***Open in New Tab*** to keep your current page open.

### *Translate a Page*

If you open a website that's in another language, Safari can translate it instantly.

1. Tap the ***Page Options*** button 🖳 in the address bar.
2. Tap ***Translate*** (for example, *Translate to English*).

***Tip:*** If you don't see this option, go to ***Settings → Safari → Translate*** and turn it on once.

### *Fill Forms Quickly with AutoFill*

Safari can automatically fill in your ***name***, ***address***, ***credit cards***, and ***passwords*** — so you type less.

To use AutoFill:
1. Tap a form field (like Name or Email).
2. Safari suggests info from your Contact card or saved details.

To turn AutoFill on or off:
1. Go to ***Settings → Safari → AutoFill***.
2. Turn on ***Use Contact Info*** and choose your name under My Info.
3. To add a saved credit card, go to ***Saved Credit Cards → Add Credit Card***.

Passwords are managed in the ***Passwords app***, and Safari can also suggest strong ones when you create a new account.

### Manage Your Tabs

**View All Open Pages:**
- Tap the **Tabs button** ⧉ at the bottom or top of the screen.

**Open a Link in a New Tab:**
- Touch and hold a link → tap **Open in New Tab**.

**Keep Reading Your Current Page:**
- Go to **Settings → Safari → Open Links → In Background**.

**See a Tab's History:**
- Touch and hold the **Back ‹** or **Forward ›** button to view previous pages for that tab.

**Close Tabs:**
- Open **More Options** •••, then select All Tabs.
- Open **All Tabs**, then tap the **Close** ⓧ button on each one.
- To close everything at once, touch and hold **Done**, then tap **Close All [number] Tabs**.

**Tip:** You can group tabs by topic. Tap **Tabs → + New Tab Group** and give it a name like "Recipes" or "Travel Plans."

### Try Other Browsers

Safari is fast, private, and built right into iOS 26. But if you prefer, you can download other browsers such as **Google Chrome**, **Firefox**, or **Microsoft Edge** from the **App Store**. They work in a similar way, and you can set your favorite one as the default browser in **Settings → Default Browser App**.

With these steps, you can browse, search, and explore safely using Safari. Whether you're using an iPhone 17 or another model with iOS 26, you'll find browsing the web simple, secure, and fast.

Your iPhone and Safari include built-in tools that help you browse the internet safely. These features keep your activity private, protect you from online trackers, and give you full control over which sites can access your data.

### Private Browsing

Private Browsing lets you visit websites without saving your history, cookies, or searches. It also turns off Safari extensions by default, keeping your activity more private.

### Open Private Browsing
1. Open **Safari**.
2. Tap **More**.
3. Open **All Tabs** (or tap the **Tabs** button if you use the bottom or top tab layout).
4. Swipe right on the tab bar until **Private** appears.
5. Tap **Unlock** and use **Face ID**, **Touch ID**, or your **passcode**.

### Exit Private Browsing
1. Tap **More** → **All Tabs**.
2. Swipe left to return to your regular tab group.
3. Safari locks your private tabs automatically when you leave.

### Lock Private Tabs with Biometrics
To make sure only you can open Private Browsing:

- Go to **Settings** → **Safari**.
- Turn on **Require Face ID | Touch ID | Passcode to Unlock Private Browsing**.

***Use a Different Search Engine in Private***
1. Go to **Settings → Safari**.
2. Turn off **Also Use in Private Browsing**.
3. Tap **Private Search Engine** and choose another option like **DuckDuckGo** or **Ecosia**.

***Tip:*** Safari extensions are small tools that add extra features, like ad blocking or translation. If you want an extension to work in Private Browsing, open **Safari → Page Menu** ▤ **→ More → Extensions Settings** and turn it on there.

### Privacy Report

Safari automatically blocks known trackers and hides your IP address — a unique number that identifies your device on the internet. You can check this at anytime.

To view your Privacy Report:
1. While in Safari, tap the **Page Menu** ▤ next to the address bar.
2. Tap **More → Privacy Report**.

You'll see how many trackers Safari has blocked and which sites attempted to track your activity.

### iCloud Private Relay (with iCloud+)

**iCloud+** is Apple's upgraded cloud service that adds features like **Private Relay**, **Hide My Email**, and **expanded iCloud storage** for backups, photos, and files. If you subscribe to **iCloud+**, you can turn on **Private Relay** for extra protection. It hides your IP address and encrypts your browsing data so websites and networks can't track you.

To turn it on or off:
1. Go to **Settings → [your name] → iCloud → Private Relay**.
2. Choose whether to use it for all networks or only for Wi-Fi and cellular.

To temporarily show your IP for a trusted site:

- In Safari, tap the **Page Menu → More → Show IP Address**. Your IP address hides again when you leave or close the tab.

**Note:** Private Relay may not be available in all regions.

### Key Safari Privacy and Security Settings

You can adjust these privacy options anytime. Go to **Settings → Safari**, then check the following:

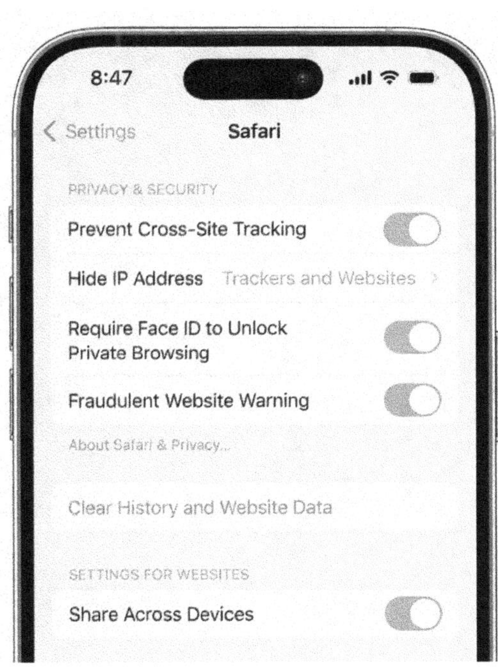


- **Prevent Cross-Site Tracking:** Keep this on to block cookies and trackers between websites.
- **Hide IP Address:** Choose **From Trackers** (standard) or **From Trackers and Websites** (with iCloud+).
- **Fraudulent Website Warning:** Keep this on to get alerts for suspicious or unsafe sites.
- **Camera / Microphone / Location:** Choose **Ask**, **Deny**, or **Allow** depending on the site.

For a specific website:

- Open the site in Safari.
- Tap **Page Menu → More → Website Settings For**.
- Adjust permissions like Camera, Microphone, or Location access.

### Safe Browsing Tips

- Use **Private Browsing** when you're on a shared or public device.
- Keep **Prevent Cross-Site Tracking** and **Fraudulent Website Warning** turned on.
- Check the **Privacy Report** on unfamiliar websites.

- Try ***Private Relay (iCloud+)*** for stronger protection on public Wi-Fi.
- Set ***Camera***, ***Microphone***, and ***Location*** permissions to ***Ask*** unless you fully trust the site.

With these tools, Safari helps you stay safe online. Whether you're reading the news, shopping, or researching, iOS 26 gives you control — so you can browse with confidence and keep your personal information private.

Make your iPhone easier to see, hear, and use — your way. This section gives you a clear tour of the most helpful accessibility features in iOS 26, what they do, and where to find them.

### *Quick Start: Where Everything Lives*
- Go to *Settings → Accessibility*.

You'll see sections for *Vision*, *Hearing*, *Speech*, and *Physical & Motor* (plus helpful tools under "General").

- *Fast access anytime:* Set up an *Accessibility Shortcut* (triple-click the Side Button).
  - Go to *Settings → Accessibility → Accessibility Shortcut →* choose your favorites (for example: VoiceOver, Magnifier, Live Speech, Sound Recognition).
- *Even faster:* Add controls to Control Center (Magnifier, Hearing, Text Size).
  - Go to *Settings → Control Center → Add* the controls you want.
- *Action Button:* You can map *Accessibility* to the Action button for one-press access.
  - Go to *Settings → Action Button → Accessibility →* pick a feature.

### *Vision Features*

 *VoiceOver*
- *What it does:* It speaks what's on screen and lets you navigate with gestures, a keyboard, or a Braille display.
- *To turn on:* Go to *Settings → Accessibility → VoiceOver* (try *VoiceOver Practice* to learn gestures).
- *Quick toggle:* Triple-click the Side Button (if set in Accessibility Shortcut).

### 👆 *Braille Display Settings*

- Go to **Settings › Accessibility › VoiceOver › Braille**.
- ***Core setup:***
  - ***Match Input & Output Tables:*** Keep Braille input and output in the same table.
  - ***Input & Output / Braille Tables:*** Pick language, six-dot or eight-dot, contracted/uncontracted; add extra tables to the rotor.
  - ***Braille Screen Input:*** Choose how you type Braille on the touchscreen.

### 💬 *Spoken Content*

- ***What it does:*** Hear text read aloud even when VoiceOver is off. It can also speak typed characters or words.
- ***To find it:*** Go to **Settings → Accessibility → Spoken Content**.
- ***Try this:*** Turn on **Speak Screen**, then swipe down with two fingers from the top of the screen to read the page.

### 📄 *Accessibility Reader*

- ***What it does:*** Makes text easier to read in many apps — adjust font, spacing, and listen to the text.
- ***To find it:*** Go to **Settings → Accessibility → Spoken Content/ Accessibility Reader** (then use it in supported apps).

### 💬 *Audio Descriptions*

- ***What it does:*** It plays spoken descriptions of visual action in supported movies and TV shows.
- ***To find it:*** Go to **Settings → Accessibility → Audio Descriptions**.

### 🔍 *Magnifier*

Use your phone like a magnifying glass.

- ***What it does:*** Zoom in on menus, labels, tiny print, and detect objects.
- ***To open:*** Use the **Magnifier** app or add **Magnifier** 🔍 to Control Center.
- ***Tip:*** Map Magnifier to the **Action Button** or Accessibility Shortcut for

instant use.

## ⊕ *Zoom*

- ***What it does:*** Enlarge part or all of the screen and pan around.
- ***To find it:*** Go to ***Settings → Accessibility → Zoom***.
- ***Hover Typing:*** Show large text for what you're typing (***Settings → Accessibility → Zoom → Hover Typing***).

## A A *Make Text & Display Easier to See*

- ***Bigger or Bold text:*** Go to ***Settings → Accessibility → Display & Text Size → Larger Text, Bold Text***.
- ***Reduce motion or flashing:*** It makes screen effects simpler and dims flashing lights. Go to ***Settings → Accessibility → Motion → Reduce Motion, Dim Flashing Lights***.
- ***Vehicle Motion Cues:*** It shows moving dots on the screen to help reduce motion sickness. Go to ***Settings → Accessibility → Motion → Vehicle Motion Cues***.

### *Hearing Features*

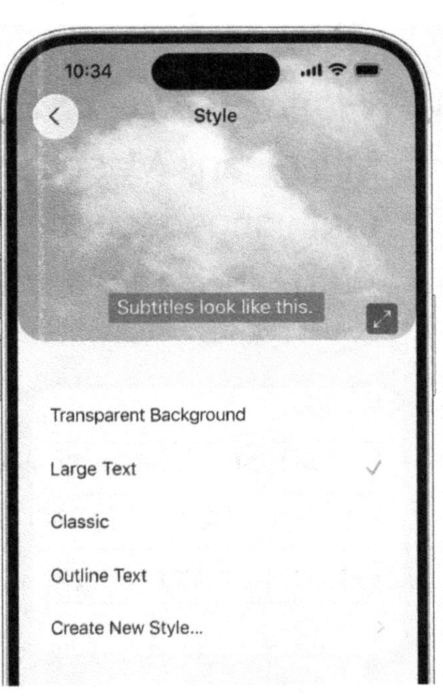


## ⌨ *Live Captions*

- ***What it does:*** Real-time on-device captions for audio from apps and in-person conversations.
- ***To find it:*** Go to ***Settings → Accessibility → Live Captions*** (then toggle it on).

## 💬 *Subtitles & Captioning*

- ***What it does:*** Customize subtitle look; use ***Closed Captions and SDH*** when available.
  - ***Closed Captions (CC):*** On-screen text you can turn on or off. It shows ***spoken dialogue plus*** important non-speech sounds — like [music], [applause], [door slams] — and often identifies who's speaking. Helpful

if you're deaf, hard of hearing, or watching with the sound off.

  - ○ **SDH (Subtitles for the Deaf and Hard of Hearing):** Similar to CC, but styled like regular subtitles. They include dialogue, speaker labels, and sound cues, and are often used in movies and streaming platforms worldwide.
- **To find it:** Go to **Settings → Accessibility → Subtitles & Captioning**.

## Sound Recognition and Name Recognition

- **What it does:** The iPhone listens for important sounds (like a doorbell or siren) and can **recognize your name** and alert you.
- **To find it:** Go to **Settings → Accessibility → Sound Recognition** (configure sounds and Name Recognition).

## Music Haptics

- **What it does:** Feel music as taps or vibrations synced with the audio.
- **To find it:** Go to **Settings → Accessibility → Music Haptics**.

## Hearing Devices & AirPods

### MFi Hearing Aids or Sound Processors

- MFi means *Made for iPhone* — these are Apple-certified hearing devices that connect directly to your iPhone.
- With MFi devices, you don't need extra accessories or streamers.

To set up:

1. Open **Settings → Accessibility → Hearing Devices**.
2. Select your hearing aids or sound processor.
3. Once paired, you can:
   - ○ Stream calls, music, and videos directly.
   - ○ Adjust programs, presets, and volume right from your iPhone.
   - ○ Check battery status.
   - ○ Use **Live Listen**, which turns your iPhone into a remote microphone.

***Note:*** If your device isn't MFi, pair it in ***Settings → Bluetooth***, or use the manufacturer's companion app for controls.

### Live Listen with Hearing Devices or AirPods
1. Go to ***Settings → Control Center →*** add ***Hearing***.
2. Open ***Control Center*** and tap the ***ear icon (Hearing)***.
3. Turn on ***Live Listen*** — your iPhone microphone will stream sound to your hearing device or AirPods.

### AirPods Special Features
- Go to ***Settings → Accessibility → AirPods***.
- Options include ***Conversation Boost*** (makes voices clearer) and other hearing-focused tools.

### Audio Balance/Mono
- Go to ***Settings → Accessibility → Audio/Visual*** to adjust left/right balance or enable mono audio.
  - ***Audio Balance*** lets you adjust sound levels between the left and right ears.
  - ***Mono Audio*** combines both stereo channels so the same sound plays in each ear — useful if you have hearing loss in one ear.

### Visual Alerts & RTT
- ***LED Flash for Alerts:*** Go to ***Settings → Accessibility → Audio/Visual → LED Flash for Alerts***.
- ***RTT/TTY calls:*** Go to ***Settings → Accessibility → RTT/TTY***.
  - ***RTT (Real-Time Text):*** Sends text live during a phone call — the other person sees each character as you type. No special hardware is needed. Great for deaf/hard-of-hearing or speech-limited users, and it can be used alongside voice.
  - ***TTY (Teletypewriter / Text Telephone):*** An older system that sends text over phone lines, typically with a ***physical TTY device*** (and carrier support). It's mainly kept today for compatibility with relay services and

older equipment.

### ⊗ *Type to Siri*

- ***What it does:*** Ask Siri by typing instead of speaking.
- ***To find it:*** Go to **Settings → Accessibility → Siri → Type to Siri**.

## *Speech & Communication*

### *Live Speech*

- ***What it does:*** Type what you want to say and have your iPhone speak it aloud (with quick-access phrases).
- ***To find it:*** Go to **Settings → Accessibility → Live Speech**.
- ***Quick access:*** Add to Accessibility Shortcut or the Action Button.

### *Personal Voice*

- ***What it does:*** Create a private, synthesized voice that sounds like you (for use with Live Speech).
- ***To find it:*** Go to **Settings → Accessibility → Personal Voice** (follow the guided recording).

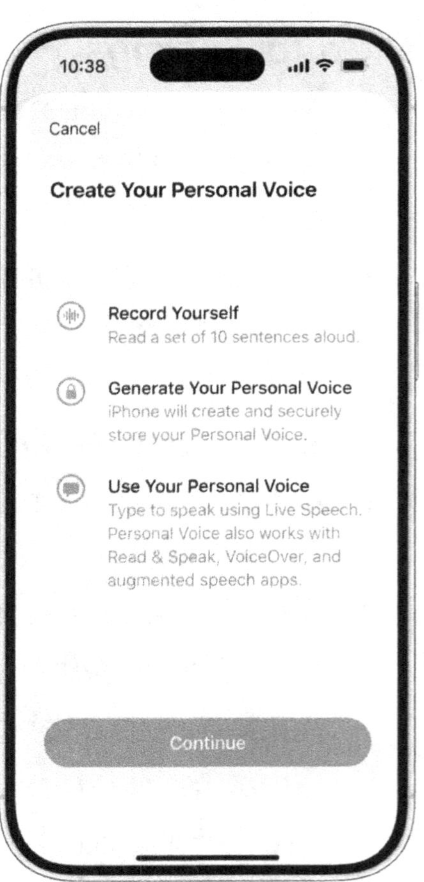


### *Voice Control*

- ***What it does:*** Navigate your iPhone and dictate or edit text using voice commands.
- ***To find it:*** Go to **Settings → Accessibility → Voice Control** (view **Commands** and add your own).

### *Vocal Shortcuts & Sound Actions*

- ***Vocal Shortcuts:*** Trigger actions when you speak a chosen word or sound.
- ***To find it:*** Go to **Settings → Accessibility → Vocal Shortcuts**.
- ***Sound Actions (Switch Control):*** Use simple sounds (like an "s" or a

mouth pop) to control your iPhone.

- **To find it:** Go to **Settings → Accessibility → Switch Control → Sound Actions**.

###  Siri for Atypical Speech

- **What it does:** Help Siri better understand atypical speech patterns.
- **To find it:** Go to **Settings → Accessibility → Siri** (adjust recognition and **Siri Pause Time**).

## Cognitive Support

### Assistive Access

- **What it does:** A simplified iPhone mode with large buttons and essential apps — great for someone you care for.
- **To find it:** Go to **Settings → Accessibility → Assistive Access** (guided setup).

### Guided Access

- **What it does:** It keeps your iPhone locked to a single app — useful for kids or when you want to focus on just one task.
- **To find it:** Go to **Settings → Accessibility → Guided Access** (set a passcode or Face ID).

### Tips

- Try **one change at a time** — use your iPhone for a day and see how it feels.
- **Pair features** that work well together (for example, Larger Text and Bold Text, or Live Captions and LED Flash Alerts).
- Keep **Accessibility Shortcut** set to your top one or two tools so help is always one triple-click away.

With these iOS 26 tools, your iPhone adapts to you — not the other way around. Pick the features that match your needs today, and adjust anytime as your needs change.

# 8. APPLE SPECIALS

## 8.1 APPLE INTELLIGENCE

Apple Intelligence helps your iPhone running iOS 26 do more for you. It can create images from short ideas, build custom emojis, translate live conversations, and understand what's on your screen so you can act faster. It also works with Siri and Writing Tools through the ChatGPT extension.

Apple Intelligence is available on all iPhone 17 models, the iPhone 16 series, and the iPhone 15 Pro or iPhone 15 Pro Max, and it will expand to more devices in future iOS 26 updates.

### Getting Started
1. Open **Settings**.
2. Tap **Apple Intelligence & Siri**.
3. Turn on **Apple Intelligence**.

### Image Playground Basics
You can create original images in seconds with the **Image Playground app**. You can also use the app inside Messages.

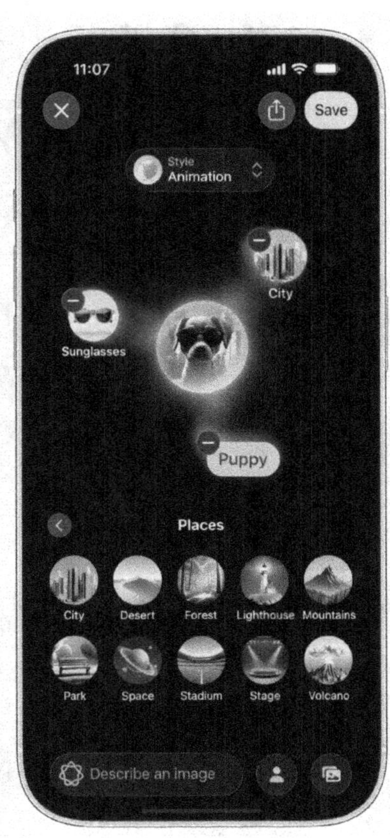

### Create or Edit an Image
1. Open the **Image Playground** app.
2. Tap **New Image**. Or tap an image and tap **Edit**.
3. Add up to seven elements:
   - **Concepts** such as themes or places.
   - **Describe an image** to type what you want.
   - **Choose Person** to use someone from your Photos.
   - **Photo Browser** to use a pet or an object.
   - **Style** to pick Animation, Illustration, or Sketch.

You can also create *Genmoji* here, a personalized animated emoji that looks like you.

4. Tap a preview to see variations. Remove items with ***Delete***.
5. Tap ***Save***. Your image goes to your gallery. Tap Done when you edit an older image.

## Customize a Person's Appearance

1. In Image Playground, tap ***New Image***.
2. Tap ***Choose Person***, then ***Edit***.
3. Pick another photo, or tap ***Customize Appearance*** to change hair, facial hair, or eyewear.
4. Add details in ***Additional Details*** if needed.
5. Tap ***Done***.

## Copy, Share, or Save

- Open an image in the ***Photos*** app.
- Tap ***More*** ••• to ***Copy*** or ***Duplicate***.
- Tap ***Share*** ⬆ to send, or ***Save Image*** to Photos.
- To delete, open the image and tap ***Delete***.

## Use Image Playground in Messages

1. Open ***Messages***. ◯
2. Open a chat.
3. Tap the ***Apps*** button ⊕, then tap ***Image Playground***.
4. Tap ***Create*** to make a new image or tap ***Gallery*** to reuse one.
5. Tap ***Send***. ⬆

## Genmoji Basics

Create your own emoji from ideas or from people in your Photos.

## Create a Genmoji

1. Open an app (like Messages ◯ ) where you can type.
2. Tap a text field.

3. Open the **emoji** keyboard by tapping 😊 or 🌐.
4. Tap **Genmoji** at the top right.
5. Add elements:
   ○ Pick **Concepts** such as expressions or costumes.
   ○ Add **Existing emoji**.
   ○ **Describe a Genmoji**.
   ○ **Choose Person** from Photos or set an appearance from scratch.
6. Tap the preview to see variations. Remove items with **Delete**.
7. Tap **Done**. Your Genmoji saves with your stickers.

## Delete a Genmoji
1. Open the **emoji** keyboard, then **Stickers**.
2. Touch and hold a Genmoji.
3. Tap **Delete**.


## Live Translation Across Apps


## Translate Text in Messages ⊙
- When a message arrives in another language, tap the chat name.
- Tap **Translate From** or **Translate To**.
- Tap **Translating ...** at the bottom to see the original or to stop translation.


**Tip:** You may be asked to download the language before starting. You will need to have an internet connection for the download to work.


## See Translated Captions in FaceTime 📹
1. During a one-on-one call, tap the screen.
2. Tap **More** ••• , then **Live Captions** to see captions with translation.

### Translate During Phone Calls

1. During a call, tap **More** ⬤⬤⬤ , then **Live Translation**.
2. Choose the caller's language and your language.
3. Tap **Start Translation**.

### Visual Intelligence

Learn more about what is around you. You can also interact with what's on your screen.

### Use the Camera to Get Details

(Only applicable to iPhone 17 models.)

1. Press and hold the **Camera Control** button (on the side of your phone).
2. Point the camera at a place or object.
3. Tap results at the top to:
   - View store hours or a menu.
   - Reserve a table or place an order.
   - Identify plants and animals.
   - Search for similar items.

### Act on Text in the Real World

1. Press and hold the **Camera Control button** on the side of your phone.
2. Point at a sign or document.
3. Tap **Summarize**, **Translate**, or **Read Aloud**.
4. Tap phone numbers, email addresses, dates, or links to call, email, create an event, or open a site.

### Use Visual Intelligence on Your Screen

1. Press the **Side Button** and the **volume up** button o take a screenshot.
2. Use the tools at the bottom to:
   - **Search** the web for similar items.

- ○ ***Ask*** a question with ChatGPT if it's turned on.
- ○ ***Add to Calendar***.
- ○ ***Summarize*** or ***Read Aloud***.
3. Save or delete the screenshot.

### *Using ChatGPT with Apple Intelligence*

ChatGPT is a smart helper from OpenAI. It answers questions and writes text in plain language. You can use it to summarize notes, explain ideas, translate short texts, or suggest replies. You choose when to use the ChatGPT extension. You can use it without an account or sign in to your ChatGPT account for a personalized experience.

### *Set up the ChatGPT Extension*

1. Open ***Settings → Apple Intelligence & Siri → ChatGPT***.
2. Tap ***Set Up***.
3. Pick ***Enable ChatGPT*** or ***Use ChatGPT with an Account***.
4. To send requests without prompts, turn off ***Confirm ChatGPT Requests*** later. This setting controls whether Siri asks before it uses ChatGPT.
   - ○ ***When it is on***, Siri asks, "Do you want to use ChatGPT?" before it sends your request.
   - ○ ***When it is off***, Siri sends your request to ChatGPT right away. You save a step. You still get asked before any photo or file is sent. This protects your privacy.

### *Compose with Writing Tools*

1. While typing a message or email, tap the ***Writing Tools*** button. 
2. Swipe up and tap ***Compose***.
3. Describe what you need, then tap ***Send***.
4. Tap ***Rewrite***, pick a suggestion, or ***Revert*** if you change your mind.

### Ask ChatGPT with Visual Intelligence

1. Press and hold **Camera Control**.
2. Point at an object.
3. Tap **Ask** to send a question to ChatGPT.
4. Type or dictate a follow-up.

### Use Siri to Get Answers from ChatGPT

- Say a request that mentions ChatGPT.
  - "Hey Siri, ask ChatGPT to summarize this document."
  - "Siri, ask ChatGPT what I can cook with these" (with a photo open).
- Siri will ask to use ChatGPT when needed. You confirm before any photo or file is shared.

### Turn off the ChatGPT Extension

- Go to **Settings → Apple Intelligence & Siri → ChatGPT**. Turn off **Use ChatGPT**.
- You can also block access in **Screen Time**. (Learn more about screen time in Section 10, *Navigate Smartly, Use CarPlay, and Do More.*)
  - Open **Settings → Screen Time**.
  - Tap **App Limits** or **Content & Privacy Restrictions**.
  - Add **ChatGPT** to the blocked list or set a time limit (zero minutes).

This way, ChatGPT can't be accessed at all, even if the extension is on.

### Privacy Notes

- When you use the extension, your request and necessary details are sent to ChatGPT. Your IP address is hidden, but a general location is shared for safety and legal reasons.
- If you don't sign in, ChatGPT does not receive your Apple account information and will not store your requests unless required by law.
- If you do sign in, your ChatGPT account rules apply.

Apple Intelligence adds helpful tools to your iPhone running iOS 26. You can create images and Genmoji, translate calls and messages, and interact with text or photos on your screen or in the real world. You can also use the ChatGPT extension with Siri and Writing Tools for extra help when you need it. Turn these features on in Settings and follow the steps in this section to explore what Apple Intelligence can do.

# 8.2 APPLE PAY

Apple Pay lets your iPhone make fast and secure payments — in stores, in apps, and on the web. You can pay without taking out your wallet, and your actual card numbers are never stored on your iPhone or shared with stores. Each payment uses a one-time security code to protect your information.

Apple Pay works on all iPhones running iOS 26. The process and screen layout may look slightly different on iPhone 17 models.

### Set Up Apple Pay (Add a Card)

1. Open the **Wallet** app.
2. Tap the **Add Card** button. ➕
3. Choose **Debit or Credit Card** (or select Apple Card, Previous Cards, or a supported bank app).
4. Follow the steps to scan or type your card details.
5. Proceed with any required verification with your bank.

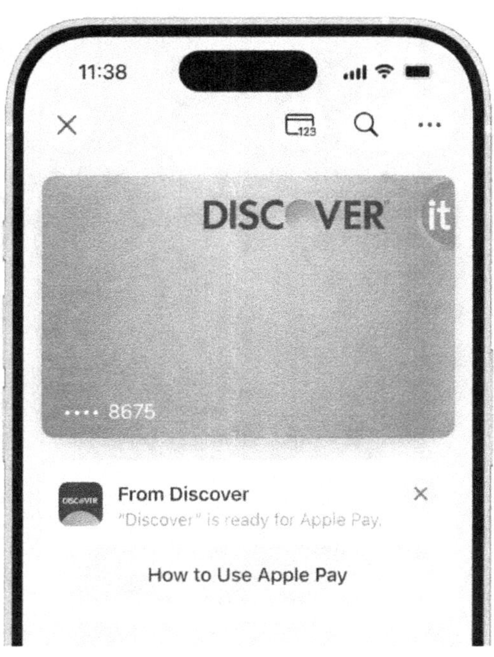


### Tips

- If your card doesn't add, check with your bank to see if it supports Apple Pay.
- If you use an Apple Watch, you'll be offered to add the same card there as well.

### Set a Recurring Payment (Apple Cash)

Apple Cash lets you send and receive money right in the Wallet app.

1. Open **Apple Cash** in **Wallet**.
2. Tap **Show Keypad**.
3. Tap **Send Recurring Payment**.

4. Pick a **_Start Date_** and how often you want to send it.

### _Manage Apple Cash_

You can view and manage your Apple Cash at anytime:

1. Open **_Wallet → Apple Cash → More_**.
2. Add money, set **_Auto Reload_**, move money to your bank, view your statements, or contact support.

### _Pay in Stores (Contactless)_

1. Double-click the **_Side Button_**.
2. Use **_Face ID_**, **_Touch ID_**, or your **_passcode_** to confirm.
3. Hold the top of your iPhone near the payment reader.
4. When you see **_Done_** ✓, the payment is complete.

All iPhones running iOS 26 support contactless payments. On iPhone 17 models, Apple Intelligence improves tap detection for faster processing.

### _Pay in Apps or on the Web_

- In Apps, App Clips, or Safari, choose Apple Pay at checkout.
- Confirm your card, shipping, and contact information.
- Approve the payment with **_Face ID_**, **_Touch ID_**, or your **_passcode_**.

On other devices like a **_Mac_** or **_Windows computer_** (on supported sites):

- Click **_Apple Pay_** at checkout.

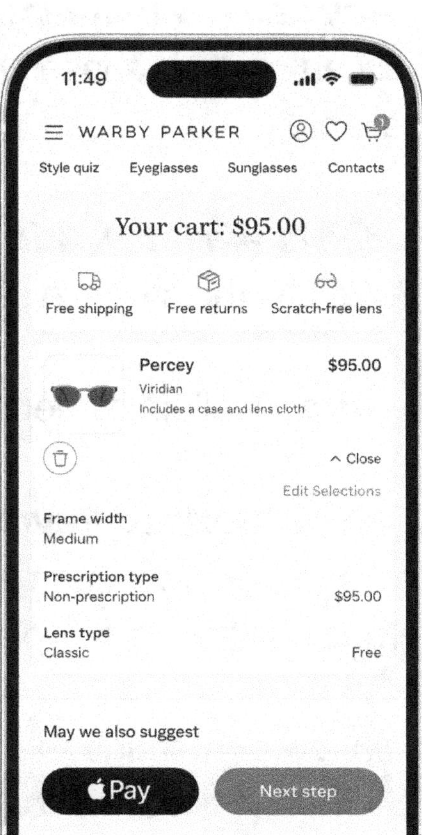

- Scan the code on your iPhone screen to confirm and pay securely.

### Manage Cards & Accounts

1. Open **Wallet** and tap a card.
2. View recent transactions (pending amounts may look slightly different from final charges).
3. Tap **Card Number** ➕ to see your device account number.
4. Tap **More** ••• ▸ for details like billing address, notifications, or to remove a card.

## Connect Your Account for More Details

Some banks let you see additional information like account balances and spending history:

- Go to **Wallet → tap the card → Get Started** (or **More → Get Account Balance & Activity**).
- Follow the steps to connect your account.

### Pay Later & Installments

You can split purchases into smaller payments with **Apple Pay Later** (where available).

1. Go to **Wallet → Add Card → Pay Later Options**.
2. Follow the steps to set up.

**Note:** Availability depends on your region and eligibility.

### Preauthorized Payments (Subscriptions & Future Charges)

Some merchants, such as streaming services or delivery apps, may ask for permission to charge your card in the future.

To review or manage them:

1. Open **Wallet → More → Preauthorized Payments**.

2. Tap any item to see when and how a merchant can charge you.
3. Tap **Revoke Payment Authorization** to stop future payments.

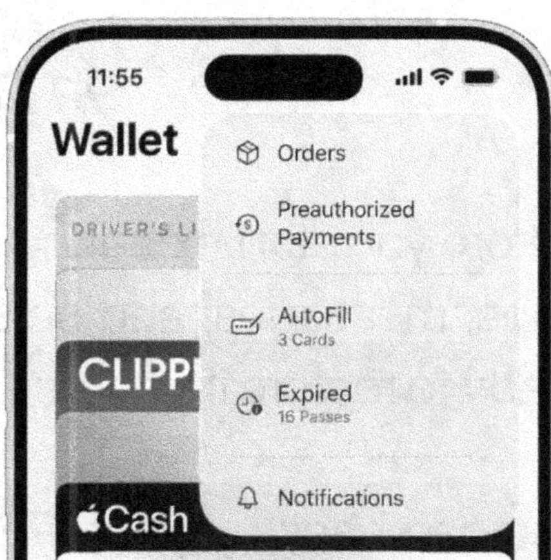

**Note:** Revoking authorization stops future payments but does not cancel the actual service. You must cancel subscriptions directly with the company.

### Apple Pay Tips

- Keep **Face ID**, **Touch ID**, or your **passcode** set up for quick payments.
- Add your card to **Apple Watch** for hands-free checkout.
- Use **Apple Cash** to send or receive money in Messages.
- Check **Settings → Wallet & Apple Pay** to manage defaults and notifications.

With Apple Pay on iOS 26, your iPhone becomes your wallet. You can tap to pay in stores, check out online, or send money in seconds — all while keeping your information private and secure.

### 9.1 DATA BACKUP AND RESTORATION

Before you start exploring your iPhone, it's important to make sure your photos, apps, messages, and settings are safe. A **backup** keeps all this information ready to restore if you lose your phone, upgrade to a new one, or need to reset it.

You can back up your iPhone to iCloud or to a **computer**. Both methods are secure and easy to use.

### *iCloud Backup: Effortless and Automatic*

iCloud is Apple's online storage system that keeps your important data in sync across all your devices. It saves your photos, contacts, messages, and other settings securely in your Apple account.

You get **5 GB of free space**, and you can upgrade to **iCloud+** if you need more. iCloud automatically backs up the parts of your iPhone that aren't already synced, such as app data, Home Screen layout, and system settings.

### *Turn on iCloud Backup*

1. Open **Settings**.
2. Tap **[your name]** → **iCloud** → **iCloud Backup**.
3. Turn on **Back Up This iPhone**.

Once enabled, your iPhone will back up **automatically every day** when it's:
- Plugged in.
- Connected to Wi-Fi.
- Locked (not in use).

**Tip:** If you have a 5G plan on a newer model

such as an *iPhone 17,* you can also turn on **Back Up Over Cellular**. This feature lets your iPhone use your mobile data to back up when Wi-Fi isn't available.

## Back Up Manually

If you want to make a backup right now:

- Tap **Back Up Now** in the same menu.

You can watch the progress bar to confirm that the backup has started.

### Back Up Using a Computer

You can also create a local backup using your Mac or Windows PC. This gives you a copy of your data stored safely offline.

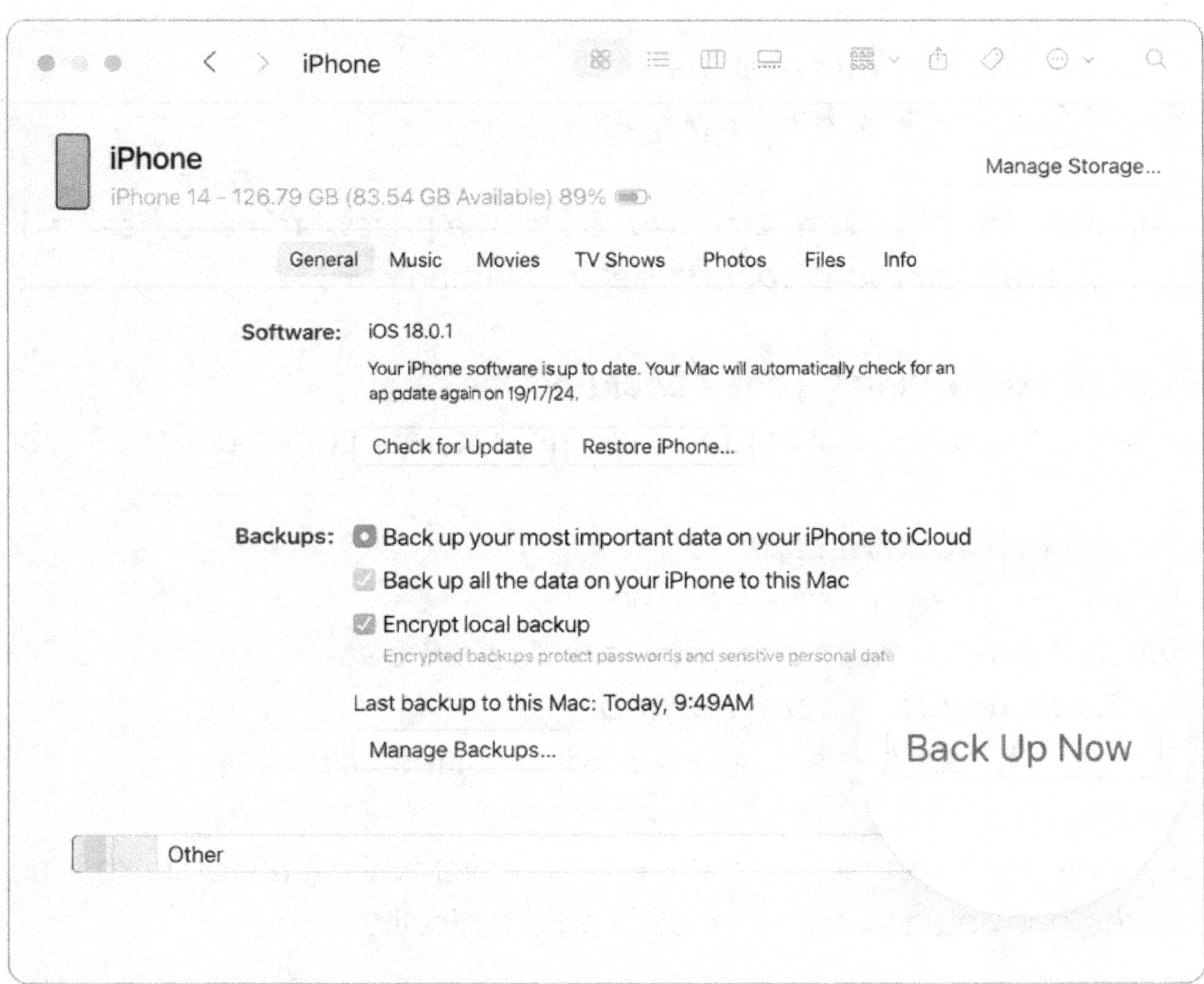

**On a Mac (macOS 10.15 or later):**
1. Connect your iPhone to your Mac using a cable (most recent iPhones use **USB-C**, so you'll need either a **USB-C to USB-C** cable for newer Macs with USB-C ports, or a **USB-C to USB-A** cable if your Mac only has the older USB-A ports).
2. Open **Finder** and select your iPhone in the sidebar.
3. Click **General**.
4. Select **Back up all of the data** on your **iPhone to this Mac**.
5. Click **Back Up Now**.

**On a PC (or an older Mac):**
1. Connect your iPhone with a **USB-C to USB-A** cable (most PCs use USB-A ports)
2. Open **iTunes** (if you don't have iTunes, download it from the Microsoft Store).
3. Click the **iPhone icon** near the top.
4. Select **Summary → Back Up Now**.

You can also **encrypt your backup** to include passwords and health data. Just check **Encrypt local backup** before starting.

### Restore Your iPhone from a Backup

If you ever replace, reset, or upgrade your iPhone, restoring your data is simple.

### Restore from iCloud Backup

1. Turn on your new or erased iPhone.
2. Follow the setup steps until you reach **Apps & Data**.
3. Tap **Restore from iCloud Backup**.
4. Sign in with your Apple ID and pick the most recent backup.

Keep your iPhone connected to Wi-Fi and power while it restores. Your apps, messages, and settings will come back automatically.

### *Restore from Computer Backup*

1. Connect your iPhone to the computer where you made the backup.
2. On a **Mac**, open **Finder**. On a **PC**, open **iTunes**.
3. Select your iPhone.
4. Click **Restore Backup**.
5. Choose the backup you want and follow the prompts.

### *Helpful Tips*

- Check your backup date regularly in **Settings** → **iCloud** → **iCloud Backup**.
- Back up before installing a major update or switching devices.
- Use **iCloud+** if you run out of space — backups can grow as you add more photos or apps.
- For extra protection, you can keep both an **iCloud** and a **computer** backup.

With iOS 26, backing up your iPhone is easier and safer than ever. Whether you use iCloud or your computer, your data stays secure — ready to restore whenever you need it.

# 9.2 Reset, Force Quit, and Update your iPhone

Even the best phones sometimes need a fresh start. Knowing how to safely reset settings, restart your iPhone if it freezes, close a stuck app, and keep iOS updated will save you stress and time. This section guides you through each process one step at a time.

### Reset iPhone Settings (Without Erasing Data)

If something feels off — like Wi-Fi not connecting, apps glitching, or Bluetooth not working — you can **reset system settings** without deleting your photos, apps, or messages.

### Steps:

1. Navigate to **Settings**, select **General**, then **Transfer or Reset iPhone**, and finally choose **Reset**.
2. Choose one of the following:
   - **Reset All Settings:** Returns all settings (Wi-Fi, Bluetooth, Notifications, Privacy, Apple Pay cards, etc.) to their defaults.

- ○ **Reset Network Settings:** Clears Wi-Fi passwords, VPNs, and cellular settings. You'll need to reconnect to Wi-Fi afterward.
- ○ **Delete All eSIMs:** Removes all eSIMs (digital SIM cards). You'll have to set up your cellular plan again.
- ○ **Reset Keyboard Dictionary:** Deletes any custom words you've added while typing.
- ○ **Reset Handwriting Style:** Restores handwriting preferences (mainly for iPhone 17 and models with Apple Pencil support).
- ○ **Reset Home Screen Layout:** Puts built-in apps back in their original spots and removes folders you created.
- ○ **Reset Location & Privacy:** Clears app permissions so apps will ask for access again next time.

*Important:* You'll also see **Erase All Content and Settings** in this menu. That completely wipes your iPhone. Use it only if you're selling, giving away, or fully erasing your device. Always back up first (see Section 9.1, *Data Backup and Restoration*).

### Using Force Restart

If your iPhone freezes or stops responding, a **force restart** can help. It doesn't delete your data — it simply restarts the device.

1. Quickly press and release **Volume Up**.
2. Quickly press and release **Volume Down**.
3. Press and hold the **Side Button** until the Apple logo appears, then release.

Your iPhone will restart normally. This process is the same on all models running iOS 26, including iPhone 17.

### Force Quitting a Frozen App

If only one app is acting up, you can close it and open it again.

1. Swipe up from the bottom of the screen and pause in the middle (to open the **App Switcher**).
2. Swipe left or right to find the app.
3. Swipe the app's preview up to close it.
4. Tap the app icon on your Home Screen to reopen it.

*Tip:* Use this method only for apps that are frozen or slow. You don't need to close apps regularly — iOS manages them automatically.

### Keeping iOS Updated

Keeping iOS up to date ensures your iPhone stays secure, stable, and ready for new features. Updates don't delete your personal data.

### Turn On Automatic Updates

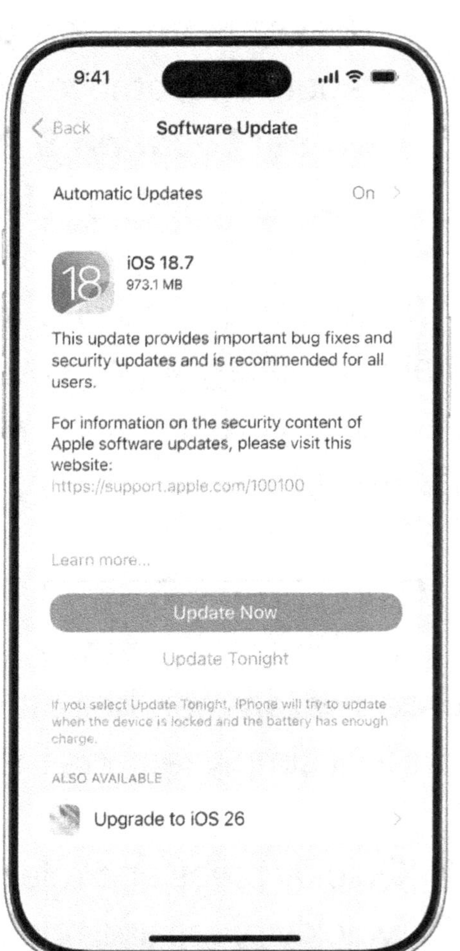

1. Go to **Settings → General → Software Update → Automatic Updates**.
2. Choose how updates install:
    - **Automatically Install:** Installs overnight while charging on Wi-Fi.
    - **Automatically Download:** Downloads updates but lets you install them later.

### Update Manually

If you prefer to do it yourself:

1. Go to **Settings → General → Software Update**.
2. Tap **Download and Install** if an update is available.

### Update Using a Computer

If you prefer a wired update or don't have enough storage:

**On a Mac (macOS 10.15 or later):**
1. Connect your iPhone to your Mac.
2. Open **Finder** and select your iPhone from the sidebar.
3. Click **General → Check for Update**, then follow the prompts.

**On a Windows PC (or older macOS):**
1. Open **iTunes** and click the **iPhone button** near the top (if you don't have iTunes, download it from the Microsoft Store).
2. Select **Summary → Check for Update**, then follow the steps.

### Update System Files Only

You can let iOS install smaller system fixes without updating the entire version.

- Go to **Settings → General → Software Update → Automatic Updates**.
  - Turn **off Automatically Install** under **iOS Updates**.
  - Turn **on Automatically Install** under **System Files**.

This keeps your iPhone running smoothly between full updates.

**Tip: Always back up first**. Before doing any reset or software update, make sure your iPhone is backed up. You can back up using **iCloud** or your **computer** (see Section 9.1, *Data Backup and Restoration*).

### Quick Fix Cheat Sheet

| Problem | Solution |
| --- | --- |
| Wi-Fi or Bluetooth not working | Reset network settings |
| iPhone completely frozen | Force restart |
| One app keeps crashing | Force quit the app |
| Slow performance or bugs | Check for iOS updates |
| Want to start fresh (no data loss) | Reset all settings |

With these tools, you can handle almost any issue — from a frozen app to a full system reset. Keeping your iPhone updated and knowing how to restart or reset it helps everything run smoothly and keeps your data safe.

Your iPhone on iOS 26 can do more than you think. It can help you stay productive, focused, and entertained — whether you're checking your commute, driving with CarPlay, or learning new features. These easy tips will help you get the most out of your day — with no stress and no confusion.

### *Maps: Smarter Navigation in iOS 26*
The **Maps** app in iOS 26 is smarter, faster, and more personal — helping you reach places quickly while respecting your privacy.

### *Preferred Routes*
Your iPhone learns your routine using on-device intelligence (not shared with Apple).

- It suggests the fastest route for frequent trips like home ↔ work.
- The **Maps widget** shows commute previews and traffic updates before you leave.
- You'll get **delay alerts** with alternate routes — even if you didn't start navigation.

**Note:** This works on all iPhones running iOS 26; iPhone 17 models calculate route predictions faster.

### *Turn Preferred Routes On or Off*
If you'd like to manage or stop route predictions:

1. Open the **Settings** app on your iPhone.
2. Tap **Apps → Maps → Location**.
3. Scroll down and toggle **Preferred Routes** and **Predicted Destinations on** or **off** as you prefer.

When these options are on, your iPhone quietly learns your regular routes to save you time. Turning them off stops Maps from showing commute suggestions or traffic alerts.

### *CarPlay: Safer Driving with Your iPhone*

CarPlay 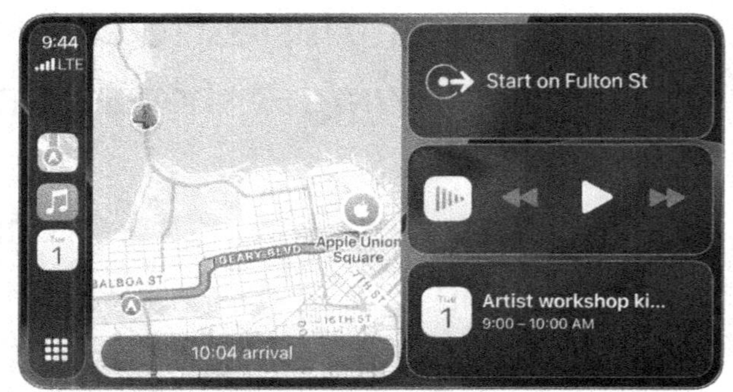 brings your iPhone's key apps to your car's built-in display, so you can drive hands-free and stay focused on the road.

With CarPlay, you can:
- Get *turn-by-turn directions* in *Maps*.
- Make and receive *calls* or *messages* with *Siri*.
- Listen to *Music*, *Podcasts*, or *Audiobooks*.
- Check your *calendar* and reminders.

### *Connect Your iPhone to CarPlay*

*If your car supports CarPlay via USB:*
1. Start your car and make sure Siri is on.
2. Plug your iPhone into the USB port (look for the CarPlay icon or smartphone icon).
3. Follow the prompts on your iPhone or car display.

*If your car supports both wireless and USB CarPlay:*
- Connect with USB once, and next time you can join wirelessly.

*If your car supports only wireless CarPlay:*
1. Press and hold your *voice command button* on the steering wheel.
2. Make sure your car stereo is in *Bluetooth or wireless mode*.
3. On your iPhone, go to *Settings → Wi-Fi*, select your car's CarPlay network, and turn on *Auto-Join*.
4. Go to *Settings → General → CarPlay*, then select your car.

### Tips

- On some ***electric vehicles***, you can use ***Maps*** to identify your car for ***EV routing***. This feature plans your route based on your car's battery and helps you find charging stops along the way.
- If CarPlay doesn't appear automatically, tap the ***CarPlay icon*** on your car's display.

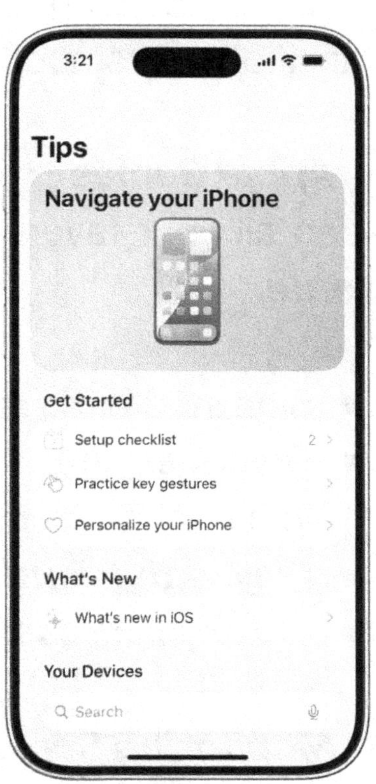

### Using Tips App

The Tips app is a built-in guide that offers short lessons and hidden tricks for your iPhone and other Apple devices.

- Open ***Tips*** ⬤ → choose a ***collection*** → tap a ***tip*** to learn more.
- ***Save a tip:*** Open the tip → tap ***Save*** 🔖 (tap again to remove).
- ***Find saved tips:*** Go back twice → tap ***Saved Tips***.
- ***Get alerts for new tips:*** Go to ***Settings*** → ***Notifications*** → ***Tips*** → ***Allow Notifications***.
- Scroll to the bottom of ***Tips*** to discover guides for iPad, Mac, and Apple Watch.

### Multitasking with Picture in Picture (PiP)

Watch videos or stay on a FaceTime call while using other apps.

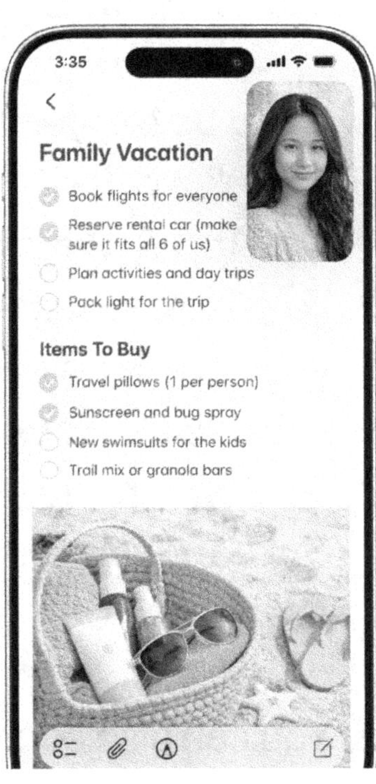

- While a video is playing, tap ***Minimize Video*** ⬒ . The video will shrink into a small window.
- ***Resize:*** Pinch open to make it bigger, pinch closed to make it smaller.
- ***Move:*** Drag the window to any corner of the screen.

- *Hide (but keep playing):* Drag it off the left or right edge.
- *Show controls:* Tap the PiP window.
- *Close:* Tap Close. ⊗
- *Return to full screen:* Tap *Restore Full Screen*. ⬃

All models running iOS 26 support Picture in Picture. On iPhone 17, playback transitions are smoother due to Apple Intelligence support.

### Apple Games

Keep all your favorite games and achievements in one place with *Game Center*.

- Sign in with the same Apple ID used in the *App Store*.
- *Discover new games:* Open *Apple Games → Home* to see recommendations.
- *Play with friends:* Go to *Friends → Challenge Your Friends*.
- *Track progress:* Open *Library* to view achievements and leaderboards.

### Monitoring Screen Time

See how much time you spend on apps and set limits for a healthier balance.

1. Go to *Settings → Screen Time → App & Website Activity → Turn On App & Website Activity*.
2. To share usage data across all your Apple devices, turn on *Share Across Devices*.
3. To view reports: Go to *Settings → Screen Time → See All App & Website Activity → choose Day or Week*.
4. You can also add the *Screen Time*

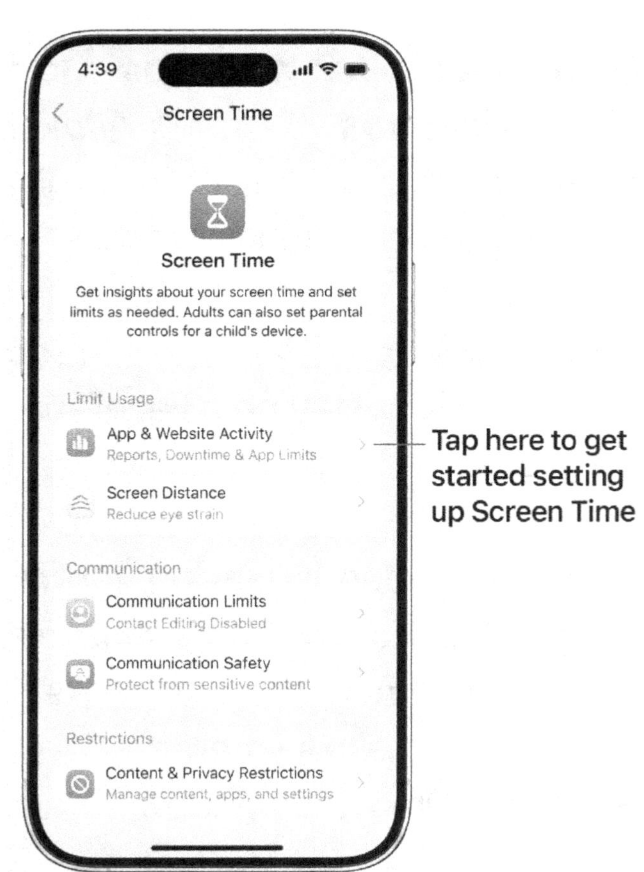

***widget*** to your Home Screen for a quick glance.

### Choose Microphone/Input per App

You can now tell each app which microphone or headset to use — perfect for recording, calls, or podcasts.

Here's how:

1. Open the app that's recording or making a call.
2. Open ***Control Center*** (swipe down from the top-right).
3. Tap the ***audio panel*** at the top (it shows the active app).
4. Tap ***Input***, then choose your source:
   - iPhone microphone (built-in)
   - Bluetooth/AirPods
   - Wired or USB-C microphone

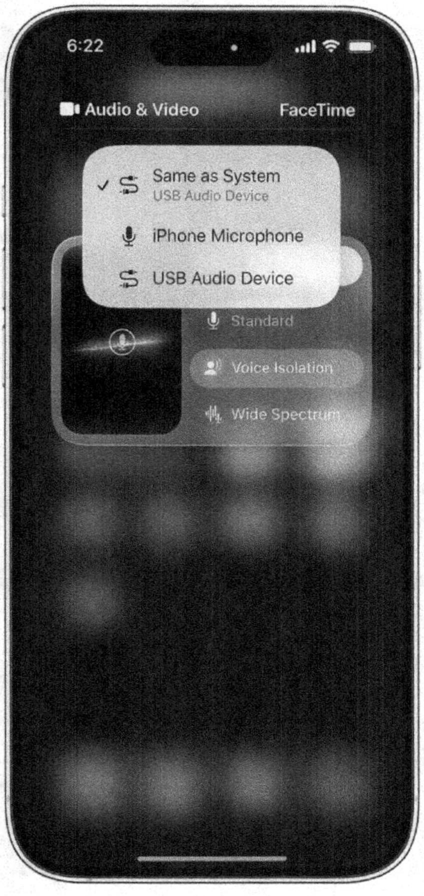


Your choice stays active for that app until you change it.

### Voice Isolation

Make your voice sound clearer on calls or recordings.

- Open ***Control Center*** → tap the ***audio panel***.
- Choose ***Voice Isolation*** to reduce background noise.
- Choose ***Wide Spectrum*** to include ambient sounds (great for group calls or music lessons). Wide Spectrum is not available in every app.

Little habits add up. Watch videos in Picture in Picture while texting, check traffic with Maps before leaving, or use Voice Isolation for clear calls. Keep Tips notifications on for daily lessons, and explore CarPlay for a safer, smarter drive.

With iOS 26, your iPhone isn't just a phone — it's your daily helper, travel guide, teacher, and co-pilot.

## *KEEP EXPLORING AND ENJOY iOS 26*

Congratulations!    You've reached the end of your ***iOS 26 User Guide for Beginners*** and learned how to make the most of your iPhone. You now know how to call and message, browse the web, take great photos and videos, download apps, pay securely with Apple Pay, stay safe with privacy tools, and keep your device running smoothly with backups and updates.

Remember, learning takes time. You don't need to know every feature right away. Keep exploring — each tap helps you grow more confident. If you forget a step, open the ***Tips app***, revisit any section in this guide, or check ***Apple Support*** for extra help.

Here are a few fun ideas to keep practicing each week:

- Customize your ***Lock Screen*** and try adding a widget.
- Create a ***Genmoji*** or design an image in ***Image Playground***.
- Link a ***Focus*** mode to your Lock Screen to reduce distractions.
- Set up ***Apple Pay*** and ***Wallet*** for quick, private payments.
- Explore ***Accessibility*** settings to make your iPhone easier to use.
- Turn on ***iCloud Backup*** and ***Find My*** for extra safety and peace of mind.

Your iPhone with ***iOS 26*** is designed to make life easier, more connected, and more enjoyable — whether you're staying in touch with loved ones, capturing memories, learning something new, or discovering the world from your pocket.

So take your time, tap around, and enjoy what your iPhone can do.

You've got this — and your journey with iOS 26 has just begun!

## A



## B



## C